ELEMENTARY MUSIC THEORY FOR ORTHODOX LITURGICAL SINGING

In Memory of

my mother,

Laura Lukashevich Barrett Butcka

(+ 2005),

and

Dedicated to

Fr Sergei Glagolev.

Elementary Music Theory

for

Orthodox Liturgical Singing

by

David Barrett

Foreward by
Father Sergei Glagolev

Orthodox Liturgical Press
Southbury, Connecticut
January 2015

Library of Congress Cataloging-in-Publication Data

Barrett, David
1956 –

Elementary Music Theory for Orthodox Liturgical Singing

Library of Congress Control Number: 2014932638

ELEMENTARY MUSIC THEORY FOR ORTHODOX LITURGICAL SINGING

Copyright © 2015 by
David Barrett

Orthodox Liturgical Press
Southbury, CT 06488

All Rights Reserved.

ISBN   978-0-9915905-0-6

Printed in the United States of America by
Lightning Source Inc.
1246 Heil Quaker Boulevard
La Vergne, TN 37086 – 3515

CONTENTS

FOREWORD — xi

PREFACE — xiii

1. MUSIC READING — 1
   - A. RHYTHM AND METER — 2
   - B. PITCH — 15
   - C. INTERVALS — 21
   - EXERCISES • CHAPTER 1 — 25
2. KEYS AND SCALES — 35
   - A. MAJOR SCALES — 35
   - B. SCALE DEGREES — 38
   - C. KEYS AND KEY SIGNATURES — 40
   - D. SOLFEGE SYLLABLES — 42
   - E. MINOR KEYS AND SCALES — 44
   - EXERCISES • CHAPTER 2 — 47

3. TRIADS 53
  A. CHORDS AND TRIADS 53
  B. QUALITIES OF INTERVALS AND TRIADS 56
  C. 7TH CHORDS 62
  D. INVERSIONS 63
  E. TRIADS IN MAJOR AND MINOR KEYS 66
  F. MUSIC ANALYSIS 68
  EXERCISES • CHAPTER 3 74

4. GIVING PITCHES 77
  A. TRIADS 79
  B. INVERSIONS 86
  C. 7TH CHORDS 87
  EXERCISES • CHAPTER 4 88

5. MELODY AND HARMONY   91
     A. MOTIVES AND PHRASES   91
     B. ANTECEDENT – CONSEQUENT PHRASES   93
     C. MONOPHONY   94
     D. DIOPHONY   96
     E. HOMOPHONY   97
     F. POLYPHONY   98
     EXERCISES • CHAPTER 5   100

6. BYZANTINE CHANT   101
     A. ESSENCE OF CHANT   101
     B. BYZANTINE CHANT AND OKTOECHOS   104
     EXERCISES • CHAPTER 6   118

7. RUSSIAN CHANT   119
     A. STIKHERA TONES   120
     B. TROPARION TONES   134
     C. PROKEIMENON TONES   147
     D. KANON TONES   156
     E. KIEVAN CHANT STIKHERA TONES   171
     EXERCISES • CHAPTER 7   186

8. CONDUCTING AND REHEARSING	187
A. BEAT PATTERNS	188
B. CHANT STYLE	192
C. STIKHERA STYLE	202
D. REHEARSALS	207
EXERCISES • CHAPTER 8	210
9. THEOLOGY OF ORTHODOX LITURGICAL MUSIC	213
A. THE HOLY TRINITY	214
B. THE TRINITARIAN DIMENSION OF ORTHODOX LITURGICAL MUSIC	217
C. MUSIC AND TEXT	218
D. LITURGICAL MUSIC AND ESCHATOLOGY	221
ANSWERS TO EXERCISES	225
BIBLIOGRAPHY	249
GLOSSARY OF TERMS	255

FOREWARD

While teaching courses in Liturgical Music at St Vladimir's Seminary years ago, David Barrett and I often enjoyed discussing the progress of sacred song and worship in the liturgical life of the Orthodox Church in America. In fact, sacred song is worship in liturgy: to pray is to sing; singing is the way we pray.

Given the importance of understanding liturgical music as prayer, we were troubled by how few choir leaders had at least an elementary grasp of music theory and practice. Music – particularly the music that is worship – has its own language that must be grasped and understood. The universal "A-B-C's" of this language is the Theory of Music that allows music to sing.

David Barrett is responding to the need of a new generation of choir leaders to understand the basic "rules" that give shape and structure to the words we sing as worship.

Fr Sergei Glagolev
East Meadow, NY
June 2013

Fr Sergei Glagolev is a renowned music teacher and composer of Orthodox liturgical music.

PREFACE

There has long been a need in the Orthodox Church for a textbook of elementary music theory for choir directors and singers. Granted, there **are** basic music reading textbooks available in various bookstores. However, most of the time, the music examples come from the world of secular music, consisting of items from the works of Bach, Beethoven, and Brahms. While this may assist in the effort towards music reading, the selections presented are not indigenous to the world of Orthodox liturgical music.

What sets this book apart is that it is written from the perspective of an Orthodox liturgical musician, singer, and choir director. Therefore, the music examples presented are culled from the various services and musical traditions of the Orthodox Church. As the student works through the various examples and exercises in the book, he or she will not only be learning to read music, but will also be simultaneously learning the music of the Orthodox liturgical tradition.

As we all learned to speak before learning to read, so the material in this book is presented for practice before the written examples appear. May God grant that the material presented herein will lead the Orthodox liturgical musician to master the skills needed to sing and give glory, worship, and thanksgiving to the Three Persons of the Holy Trinity: the Father, and the Son, and the Holy Spirit!

1
MUSIC READING

The ability to read music is strikingly similar to the ability to read words and language. Both incorporate a sign system, where a written character represents a sound or sounds, and also may express how that sound is to be executed. Both systems combine these sounds into organized forms involving syntax and contour, or shape. Hence, with language we combine the various signs called letters and punctuation into words, sentences, and paragraphs. When the sounds that these signs represent are produced (sounded), we have language. With music, we combine the various signs called notes, rests, staves, clefs, and other signs into pitches, rhythms, melodies, harmonies, and phrases. When the sounds that these signs represent are produced (sounded), we have music.

These two systems, music and language, are also similar in the way they are learned. This is a crucial element in the ability to read music, because it is precisely the order of tasks that will make music reading either an enriching experience or a dreadful confusion. When children learn to read, they first have learned how to talk. They are then taught letters as symbols for sounds that they can already produce.

In other words, the sound comes first, and then the symbol that represents that sound is associated with it. The process is the same, or should be the same, with music. Too often, music is taught as a barrage of meaningless signs onto which are tacked "meaningful" sounds. It is much easier, as with language, to learn a sound first, and then to learn the musical symbol by association.

Music involves various sounds, but it also contains periods of silence. These interchanges of sounds and silences are grouped into patterns and, unlike a painting or a statue, take place within a specific time period. The definition of **music**, then, is sound and silence organized in time.

A. RHYTHM AND METER

Just as the beating of your heart keeps you alive via its pulse, so the pulse of rhythm makes music come alive and keeps it alive. The **beat**, therefore, is a rhythmic pulse.[1] These pulses (beats) are grouped

---

[1]Christ, William; DeLone, Richard; Kliewer, Vernon; Rowell, Lewis; and Thomson, William; *Materials and Structure of Music, Volume 1*, 2nd Edition, Prentice-Hall, Inc., Englewood Cliffs, NJ, 1972 (hereafter referred to as "*Materials*"), p. 1.

Music Reading

together, so that certain pulses (beats) are stronger than others.

To see how this works, tap your foot so as to form a regular, steady rhythm. All the beats should be of equal length. Keeping this steady beat, say "Lord, have mercy" so that each of the four syllables ("Lord", "have", "mer", and "cy") falls on a beat.

The following is the musical representation of this exercise.

Example 1

This grouping of beats is called ***meter***.[2] Accented beats are referred to as strong beats, while unaccented beats are designated as weak beats. In Example 1, the word "Lord" is the strongest beat, and the syllable "mer" is the next strongest. Using "S" to represent strong beats and "w" to designate weak beats, the example would look as follows.

---

[2]Ibid, p. 2.

Example 2

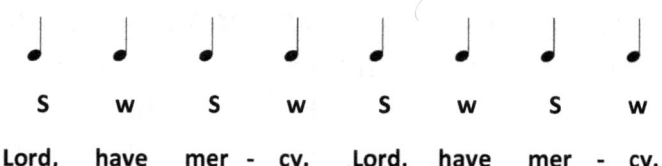

Repeat this exercise while looking at Example 2. Emphasize the strong beats, putting slightly more stress on "Lord" than on "mer". By doing this, you will see and feel a rhythmic pattern based on a cycle of four beats.

In the examples, the beats are shown by this symbol: ♩. This is called a **quarter note**.[3] Its characteristics are a blackened (filled-in) note head (•) and a stem (|). The stem can either go up or down (♩ or ♩), depending on where it occurs in the music.

A beat is understood to last until the next beat begins. Therefore, in the exercise, one beat would be the time span from the first foot tap until the next foot tap. Perform the exercise again, saying and maintaining each syllable until the next foot tap. Beginning with "Lord", hold the vowel "o" and refrain

---

[3]Ibid.

from pronouncing the "rd" until just before the following foot tap, as is illustrated below.

Example 3

This total time span from the beginning of one beat until the beginning of the next beat is called the **basic beat**, or **basic duration**.[4] Since the quarter note was used in the exercise, we say that the basic beat (basic duration) here is the quarter note. The basic beat can be of other note values, as well.

As stated earlier, by emphasizing "Lord" as the strongest beat and "mer" as the second strongest, a feeling of a rhythmic pattern based on a cycle of four beats was produced. The following illustrates this cycle metered in groups of four beats.

---

[4]Ibid.

Example 4

Each cycle of four beats is grouped into a measure. A **measure** is a grouping of the rhythmic patterns into a cycle of a specific number of beats.[5] These measures are separated by bar lines. A **bar line**, then, is the vertical line (|) which separates one measure from another.[6]

The set of numbers at the beginning of the line is called a **time signature** or **meter signature**.[7] It tells us about the cycle of beats to be used in the measures. The top number tells us how many beats are in a measure. Since the top number here is "4", there are four beats per measure. The bottom number tells us what kind of note gets one beat. Whenever the bottom number of a time signature is a "4", the quarter note is the note value which gets one beat.

---

[5]Jones, George Thaddeus, *Music Theory,* Barnes and Noble, Harper and Row, New York, NY, 1974 (hereafter referred to as "*Theory*"), p. 15.
[6]Ibid.
[7]*Materials*, p. 5.

This meter of 4/4 ("four-four") time is one of the most common meters used in Western music. It is, therefore, also known as "**common time**", and the 4/4 is often replaced with a C, meaning "common time".[8] Hence, it is from this meter of 4/4 time that the note types get their names. A quarter note, then, is called such because it takes up a quarter of a measure in 4/4 time.

Recite the "Lord, have mercy" again, giving two beats for each syllable, instead of one. Repeat the exercise a few times. Its musical representation is shown as follows.

Example 5

4/4	♩	♩		♩	♩	
	Lord,	have		mer	-	cy.

The type of note shown here is called a *half note* because it takes up half the measure in 4/4 time.[9] The half note is characterized by an open (not filled-in) note head (○) and a stem (|). Again, like the

---

[8]*Theory*, p. 19.
[9]*Materials*, p. 2. Cf.,, *Theory*, p. 12.

quarter note, it can be written with the stems either going up or down (𝅗𝅥 or 𝅗𝅥). Notice that when stems go up they are written on the right side of the note head (𝅗𝅥), but when stems go down they are written on the left side of the note head (𝅗𝅥).

When going from one measure to the next, the first beat in each measure is always counted as "1". So, in examples 5 and 6, "Lord" begins on beat 1 of the first measure, "have" begins on beat 3 of the first measure, and "mer" begins on beat 1 of the second measure.

Example 6

4/4	𝅗𝅥	𝅗𝅥		𝅗𝅥	𝅗𝅥		𝅗𝅥	𝅗𝅥	
	1 2 3 4			1 2 3 4			1 2 3 4		
	Lord,	have		mer	- cy.		Lord,	have	

Repeat the exercise, using four beats for each syllable of "Lord, have mercy". Then, sing this with the example below.

Example 7

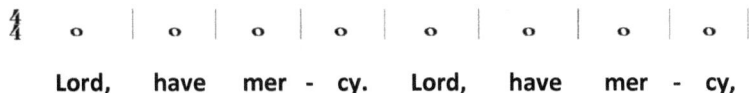

Since this note value, in 4/4 time, takes up the whole measure, it is called a **whole note**.[10] Here, a whole note gets four beats. It is recognized as an open note head with no stem (o).

Repeat the exercise again, this time singing each syllable on every half beat. In other words, begin the foot tap, then sing "Lord" when your foot is down (tapping the floor), "have" when the foot is all the way up, "mer" when the foot again taps the floor, and "cy" when the foot is again all the way up. Repeat this a few times, then continue it while looking at the following example.

---

[10]Ibid.

Example 8

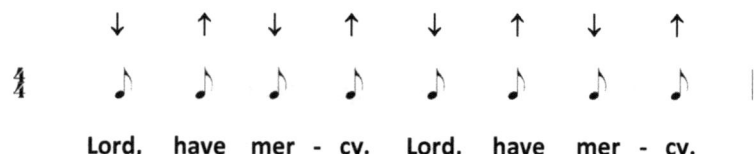

The arrows pointing down are downbeats, while those pointing up are upbeats. Notice that the point when a full beat begins is on the downbeat.

Example 9

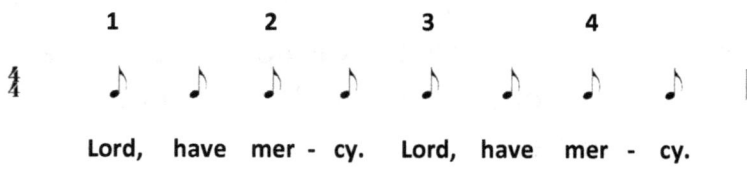

The type of note shown here is called an *eighth note*, because in 4/4 time it takes up one-eighth of a measure.[11] The eighth note consists of a blackened (filled-in) note head, a stem, and a flag (♪). Flags are

---

[11]Ibid.

Music Reading 11

always written on the right side of stems, whether the stems go up (♪) or down (♩).

To clarify music reading, flags of eighth notes that are of the same beat can be connected. To do this, they take the form of a horizontal line, as shown below.

Example 10

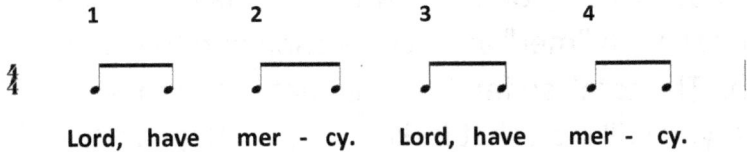

When we count eighth notes in metered music, the numbers represent the downbeats, while the "&"'s ("and"'s) signify the upbeats.

Example 11

Notes represent sound in music. To represent the silence that occurs in music, symbols called **rests** are used. Return to the exercise of chanting "Lord, have mercy", this time giving "Lord" and "have" a half beat each ("Lord" on the downbeat, "have" on the upbeat), with "mer" and "cy" getting one full beat each. The total, so far, is three beats. The fourth beat, you will rest, that is, keep silent. Repeat this exercise a few times.

Example 12

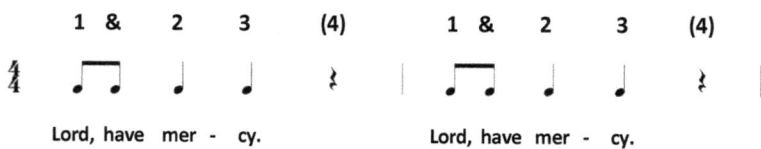

When counting using the numbers at the top of the exercise, you will not count what is not there. For example, after counting "2", you will not count "&", since there is no eighth note at this point.

The z-shaped zigzag on the fourth beat represents one beat rest in $\frac{4}{4}$ time; it can also be said that it takes up a quarter of the measure. Therefore, it is a *quarter rest*.[12] The following is a review of the note values presented, with their corresponding rest values.

A **whole note** (o) gets four beats, as does a **whole rest** (-), while looks like an upside-down hat.

A **half note** (♩) gets two beats, as does a **half rest** (-), which looks like a right side-up hat.

A **quarter note** (♩) gets one beat, as does a **quarter rest** (𝄽), which looks like a z-shaped zigzag.

An **eighth note** (♪) gets a half beat, as does an **eighth rest** (𝄾), which looks like the number 7.

As stated, the time signature of $\frac{4}{4}$ is so common it is called "common time" and can be written as C. If we use a time signature of $\frac{2}{2}$ ("two-two") time, there will be two beats per measure, with a half note getting one beat.

---

[12]Ibid.

Example 13

It is said that 2/2 time "cuts" 4/4 time in half. Therefore, it is often referred to as **cut time** or **alla breve**, and its time signature can written like this: ¢.[13]

These are examples of **strict meter**, which contain a specified number of beats per measure. Most Orthodox liturgical music makes use of **free meter**, whereby the music is organized according to the text. This will be discussed in the section on chant. The purpose, then, of examining strict meter is to become familiar with the various note and rest values used in both strict and free meters.

---

[13] *Theory*, p. 19.

B. PITCH

The second major aspect of music reading is pitch. **Pitch** is the highness or lowness of a sound resulting from vibrations per second.[14] For sound to travel, particles of matter need to vibrate. These can be particles of air, water, or solid matter. For example, when a person sings, the vocal cords vibrate together, which then set off particles of air vibrating until the sound reaches our ears, at which point we hear the sound produced. The ***frequency***, or speed of vibrations, determines the pitch. The faster the vibrations, the higher the pitch; the slower the vibrations, the lower the pitch.

Pitches are designated in the Western musical system by the first seven letters of the English alphabet: ***A***, ***B***, ***C***, ***D***, ***E***, ***F***, and ***G***. Beginning on a low ***A*** and singing up to the next ***A***, eight letter names are used, with the ***A*** repeated at the end. Therefore, the space between two notes of the same letter name is called an ***octave***.[15] All notes of the same letter name share the same relationship with each other and, therefore, sound the same. This relationship is such

---

[14]*Materials*, p. 13ff. Cf., *Theory*, p. 20ff.
[15]*Theory*, p. 15.

that a note that is an octave above has twice the vibrations per second as the starting note. For example, a particular note **C** has 573.3 vibrations per second. The **C** an octave above that one has 1,146.6 vibrations per second, which is twice 573.3. The **C** below the first one has 286.65 vibrations per second, which is half of the 573.3. This is why all pitches of the same letter name sound alike; they all share the same relationship of vibrations per second.

It would be advantageous for you to acquire access to a musical keyboard, to be able to associate the sounds with the written musical symbols that will follow. The following is an illustration of a musical keyboard.

Example 14

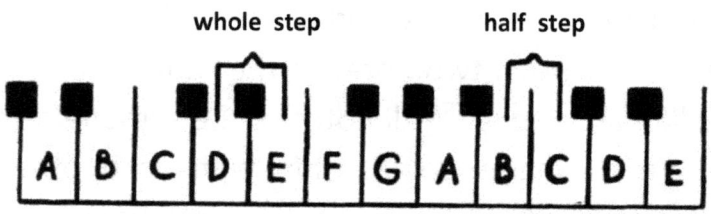

Notice that certain white keys have black keys between them. The black keys are either in groups of two or three. Going from left to right on the keyboard moves us up the musical alphabet of notes (**A**, **B**, **C**, etc.). Make note of the fact that the white key just to the left of the set of ***two*** black keys is **C**, and the white key just to the left of the set of ***three*** black keys is **F**.

Beginning on the **C** in the middle of your keyboard (using a piano will be more accurate to locating this precise **C**), play all of the white keys to the right until you come to the next **C**.

Example 15

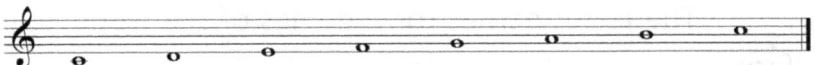

Since we are not concerning ourselves with rhythm, whole notes will be used without any time signatures. The set of five lines and four spaces between these lines is called a ***staff***.[16] Note the "**G**"-shaped symbol at the beginning of the staff. This is known both as the ***G-clef*** and the ***treble clef***.[17] It is

---

[16]*Theory*, p. 20.
[17]*Materials*, p. 13.

called a *G*-clef because, along with being shaped like the letter *G*, the curlicue loop at the bottom of the clef circles around the second line of the staff (lines and spaces are always counted from the bottom up), which is the line for the pitch *G*. It is called a treble clef because it encompasses the pitches in the treble range of voices: sopranos, altos, and (sometimes) tenors. The following are the letter names for the notes of the treble staff.

Example 16

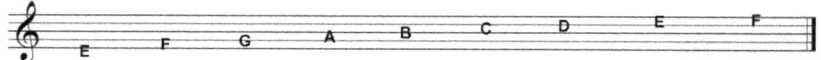

The letter names for the lines of the treble staff (going from bottom to top) are *E, G, B, D,* and *F*. A way to remember this is "*E*very *G*ood *B*oy *D*oes *F*ine". The names of the spaces are *F, A, C,* and *E*, or "*FACE*".

Returning to your keyboard, start at the *C* an octave lower than where you did before, and play the white keys until you come to the next *C*.

Music Reading

Example 17

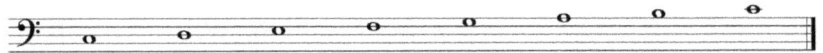

Look at the clef at the left side of this staff. It looks like a backward "**C**" with a pointed end and two dots arranged vertically. This is called both the **F-clef** and the **bass clef**.[18] It is called the **F**-clef because the line in between the two vertical dots, the fourth line of the staff, is named **F**. It is called the bass clef because it covers the bass range of voices: tenors and basses. The names of the notes of the bass staff are as follows.

Example 18

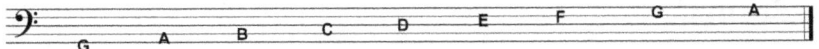

The letter names for the lines of the bass staff are **G**, **B**, **D**, **F**, and **A**. An easy way to remember this is "**G**reat **B**ig **D**ogs **F**ight **A**nimals". The names of the

---

[18]Ibid, pp. 13-14.

spaces are **A**, **C**, **E**, and **G**. To memorize this, remember that "**A**ll **C**ows **E**at **G**rass".

You may already be familiar with the treble staff, since it is used frequently to teach music reading in schools. To associate the notes of the bass staff with those of the treble staff, remember that the notes of the bass staff are one line or space lower than those of the treble staff. For example, on the treble staff, **C** is on the third space; on the bass staff, **C** is on the second space, that is, one space down. Likewise, on the treble staff, **G** is on the second line; therefore, **G** falls on the first line on the bass staff, one line down.

If we combine the treble and bass staves together ("***staves***" is the plural of "staff"), the following results.

Example 19

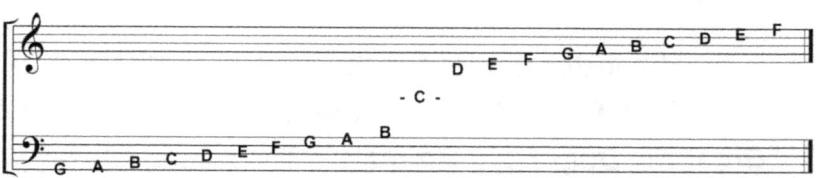

This is known as the **grand staff** or **great staff**.[19] Notice the **C** on the small line between the two staves. This is known as **middle C**, since it is in the middle of the grand staff.[20] It is on a **ledger line**, a line located above or below a staff on which to write notes.[21] Since it only appears where a note is present, the ledger line does not go across the page. Middle **C** is the top **C** for the bass staff and the lower **C** for the treble staff. This is the **C** found in the middle of a piano keyboard.

C. INTERVALS

An *interval* is the distance between two tones.[22] Numbers are used to show the size of this distance in relation to how many letter names are used. For example, **C** to **E** is a 3rd, since it encompasses three letter names for the notes: **C, D,** and **E**. When counting intervals, always count the starting note as "1".

---

[19]*Theory*, p. 21. Cf., *Materials*, p. 14.
[20]*Theory*, p. 21.
[21]Ibid, p. 22.
[22]*Theory*, p. 31. Cf., *Materials*, p. 21.

Example 20

Item 1 of example 20 shows the same note given twice. This is the interval of a 1st, or unison. Item 2 goes from **C** to **D**, so **C** is counted as "1" and **D** as "2"; therefore, **C** to **D** is an interval of a 2nd. Item 3 illustrates the aforementioned **C** to **E**, and is a 3rd. The remaining items follow this pattern. Item 8 goes from **C** to **C**; this is the interval of an 8th, or octave.

When an interval moves **down** from a given note, it is called a ***lower interval***.[23] For example, a 5th up from **C** is **G**, but a 5th **down** from **C** is **F** (**C**, **B**, **A**, **G**, **F**).

---

[23]Apel, Willi, *Harvard Dictionary of Music*, 2nd Edition, Belknap Press, Harvard University Press, Cambridge, MA, 1972 (hereafter referred to as "*Harvard*"), p. 419, under "Interval".

Example 21

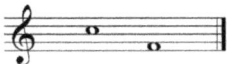

Returning to your musical keyboard, play the note **A** (refer back to example 14), then play the black key just to the left of **A**.

Example 22

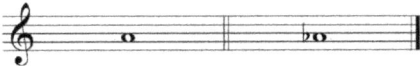

The symbol before the second note **A** in the example is a flat. A ***flat*** lowers a note by one half step.[24] Since this note is one half step lower than **A**, it is called **A-flat**, or **A**^{b}.

Play the note **F** on your keyboard, then play the black key just to the right of **F**.

---

[24]*Theory*, p. 23.

Example 23

The symbol before the second note *F* in the example is a sharp. A ***sharp*** raises a note by one half step.[25] Since this note is one half step higher than *F*, it is called ***F-sharp***, or *F#*.

Play *B* on your keyboard, then play the black key just to the left of *B* (which is *B♭*), then play the white key on *B* again.

Example 24

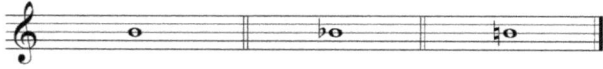

The symbol before the last note *B* is a natural sign. A ***natural sign*** cancels a sharp or a flat.[26] Since

---

[25]Ibid.
[26]Ibid.

the last note **B** has cancelled the flat by the natural sign, it is called **B-natural**, or **B♮**.

The black key for **B♭** is also right above the white key for **A**. Therefore, this **B♭** can also be called **A♯**. When two notes sound the same but have different letter names, they are called **enharmonic**.[27] Thus, **A♯** is enharmonically the same as **B♭**.

The exercises that follow will prove helpful in reinforcing the basic skills for music reading.

EXERCISES • CHAPTER 1

1. Write out the following types of notes:

A) quarter note   B) half note

C) whole note   D) eighth note

E) two eighth notes, connected

F) quarter note, half note, whole note

G) two eighth notes, separated

H) eighth note, quarter note, eighth note

I) half note, eighth note

J) whole note, eighth note, quarter note, eighth note

---

[27]Ibid, p. 24.

K) eighth note, stem down
L) two eighth notes, connected, stems up
M) two quarter notes, whole note
N) two eighth notes, separated, stems down
O) half note, whole note, half note
P) whole note, eighth note, whole note, eighth note
Q) two quarter notes, whole note
R) eighth note, two half notes, eighth note
S) two half notes, quarter note
T) whole note, half note, quarter note, eighth note

2. Write out the following types of rests:

A) whole rest
B) quarter rest
C) eighth rest
D) half rest
E) half rest, two quarter rests
F) eighth rest, whole rest, eighth rest
G) whole rest, half rest
H) two half rests
I) three quarter rests, two eighth rest
J) half rest, two quarter rests, half rest
K) eighth rest, half rest, eighth rest
L) quarter rest, whole rest, quarter rest
M) eighth rest, two quarter rests

Music Reading

N) quarter rest, half rest, two quarter rests
O) whole rest, eighth rest, half rest
P) half rest, two eighth rests, quarter rest
Q) quarter rest, two whole rests
R) two quarter rests, whole rest, eighth rest
S) two half rests, whole rest
T) whole rest, half rest, quarter rest

3. On the treble staff, write the following notes:

A) *A*
B) low *F*
C) middle *C*
D) high *E*
E) *B^b*
F) *C$^\#$*
G) low *E^b*
H) high *G*
I) low *D$^\#$*
J) *A^b*
K) high *D^b*
L) low *G^b*
M) *A$^\#$*
N) middle *C^b*
O) *B$^\#$*
P) high *E$^\#$*
Q) *B*
R) low *F$^\#$*
S) low *D*
T) high *F^b*

4. On the bass staff, write the following notes:

A) *F$^\#$*
B) low *C*
C) high *A*
D) low *A^b*
E) high *G*
F) *B^b*
G) *D*
H) low *G^b*
I) middle *C^b*
J) high *A$^\#$*
K) *D^b*
L) *F*

M) low C#   N) B   O) high G#
P) F♭   Q) D#   R) E♭
S) B#   T) E

5. Write the following intervals in relation to the given notes:

A) 4th above   B) 5th below   C) 3rd above   D) 8th above   E) 6th below

F) 7th below   G) 6th below   H) 4th above   I) 5th above   J) 5th below

K) 7th above   L) 8th below   M) 6th above   N) 4th below   O) 6th above

P) 5th above   Q) 7th below   R) 3rd above   S) 6th above   T) 4th below

Music Reading

6. Identify the following notes of the treble staff, and write its corresponding place on the bass staff:

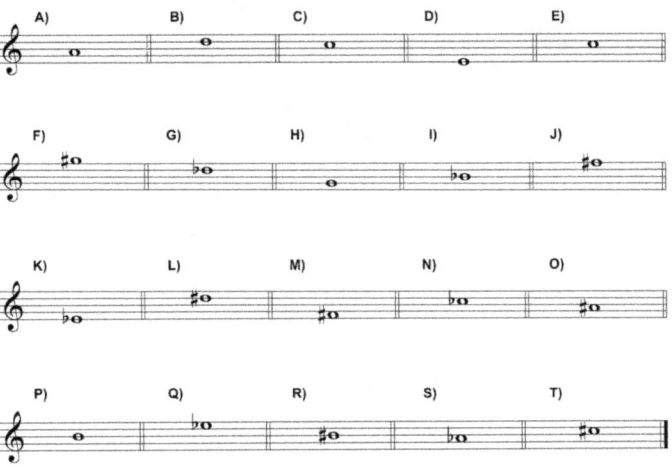

7. Identify the following notes of the bass staff, and write its corresponding place on the treble staff:

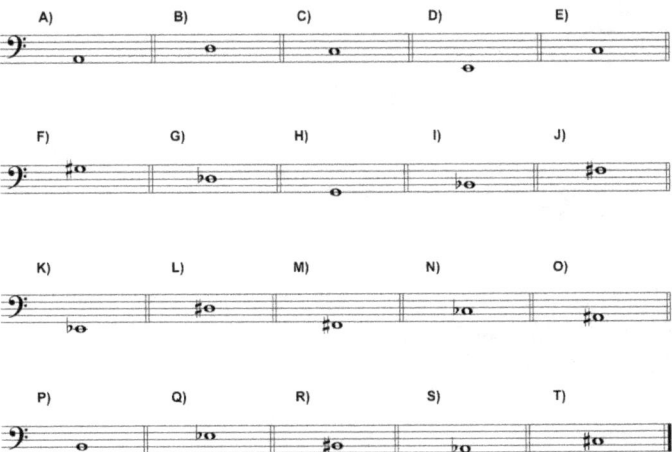

8. Name the following notes of the treble staff:

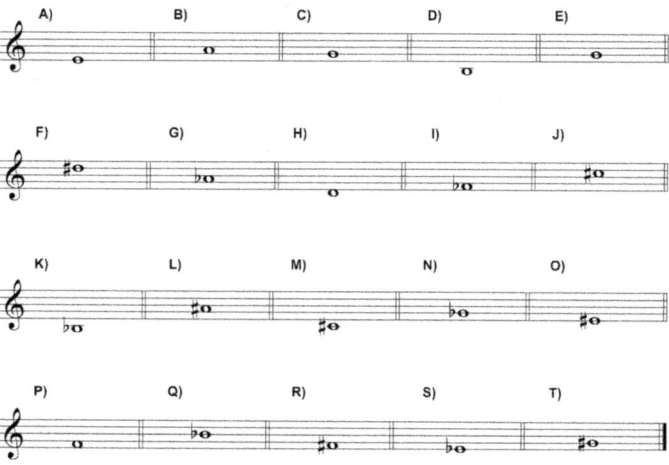

9. Name the following intervals.

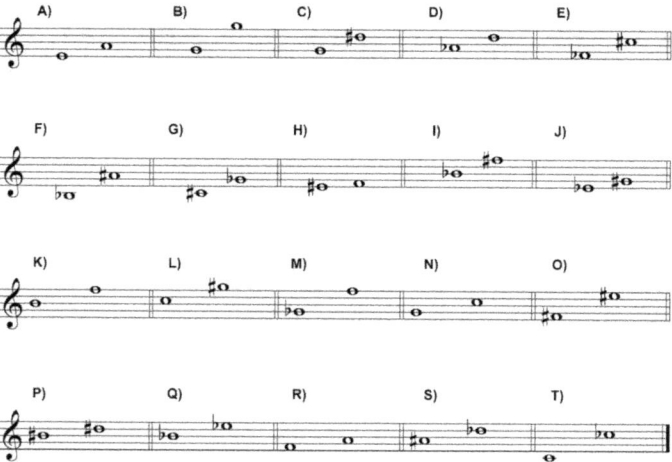

Music Reading

10. Name the following lower intervals.

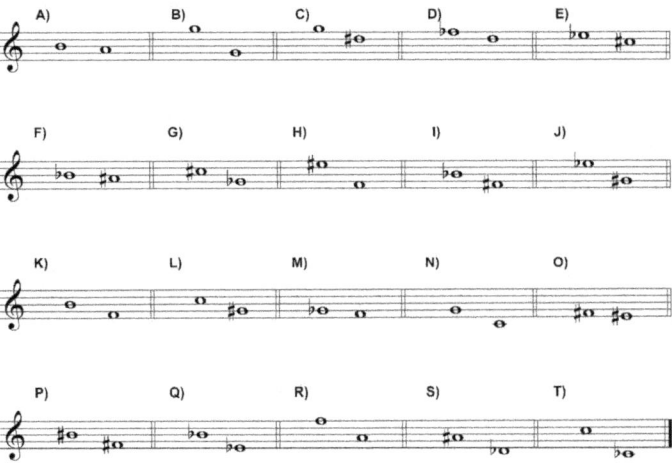

11. Fill in the following incomplete measures with the correct note value(s).

12. Fill in the following incomplete measures with the correct rest value(s).

13. Identify the notes, rests, and combinations thereof:

Music Reading

14. Identify each of the following time signatures, giving specific information about what the top number and the bottom number of each one signifies.

A) 4/4   B) 3/2   C) 3/4   D) 9/2   E) 7/8

F) 11/4   G) 13/2   H) ¢   I) 7/2   J) 3/8

K) 12/4   L) 9/8   M) 4/2   N) 8/2   O) 13/4

P) 11/8   Q) 5/4   R) 3/2   S) 5/2   T) C

15. Give the definition for each of the following.

A) music B) beat
C) meter D) quarter note
E) basic beat F) measure
G) bar line H) time signature
I) common time J) quarter rest
K) cut time L) pitch
M) frequency N) octave

O)	flat	P)	sharp
Q)	staff	R)	treble clef
S)	bass clef	T)	interval

2
KEYS AND SCALES

Having examined the basic elements of music reading, we can use these elements to build the structure of music through the use of keys and scales.

A. MAJOR SCALES

Beginning at middle **C** on your keyboard, play all of the white keys up to the next **C**, and then down the same white keys to middle **C** again.

Example 25

This is the **C** major scale. A ***scale*** is a series of ascending and descending tones arranged in a pattern.[1] It is the particular pattern used which will determine what

---

[1]*Materials*, pp. 34-41.

type of scale it is. Examining this **C** major scale, we can discover where the whole steps and half steps occur in the scale. To see where the whole steps and half steps occur on the white keys of a keyboard, refer back to Example 14 in chapter 1. Applying this pattern to the **C** major scale, the whole steps and half steps occur as follows.

Example 26

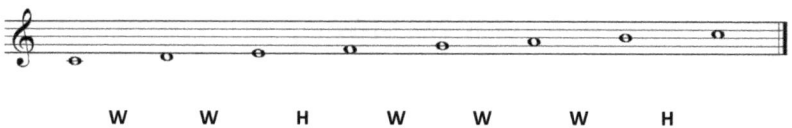

W   W   H   W   W   W   H

Between **C** and **D**, there is a whole step. This is also the case from **D** to **E**. From **E** to **F**, however, there is a half step. A whole step then occurs again from **F** to **G**, **G** to **A**, and **A** to **B**. From **B** to **C**, though, there is a half step. Thus, the pattern of whole steps and half steps for a *major* scale is: **W**hole, **W**hole, **H**alf, **W**hole, **W**hole, **W**hole, **H**alf; or **W, W, H, W, W, W, H**.[2] It is this particular arrangement of whole steps and half steps which gives a major scale its quality of being "major".

---

[2]Ibid, p. 39.

Double-check the pattern of whole steps and half steps for a major scale by examining the **F** major scale. This scale has one flat: **B♭**. Play up the keyboard, beginning on the **F** above middle **C**, remembering to play the black key just to the left of **B** for **B♭**.

Example 27

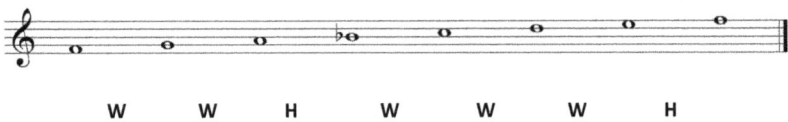

    W   W   H   W   W   W   H

Examining the **F** major scale, a whole step is found between **F** and **G**, and again between **G** and **A**. However, between **A** and **B**, a whole step occurs, at a point in the scale pattern where a half step is called for. By lowering the **B** to **B♭** (as in Example 27 above), the interval is reduced from a whole step to a half step. The next part of the pattern calls for a whole step. Between **B** and **C**, there is a half step. But, since the **B** was lowered to **B♭**, the half step is increased to a whole step: a half step between **B♭** and **B**, and another half step between **B** and **C**. Therefore, **B♭** to **C** is a whole step, as is **C** to **D**, and **D** to **E**. **E** to **F** is a half step, which is what the pattern for a major scale calls for here. So, the **F** major scale, **with its B♭**, satisfies the pattern for a major scale of **W, W, H, W, W,**

W, H. Play the **F** major scale again on your keyboard. The **pattern** of notes sounds the same as that for the **C** major scale, because the pattern of whole steps and half steps is the same.

B. SCALE DEGREES

Play again the **C** major scale ascending.

Example 28

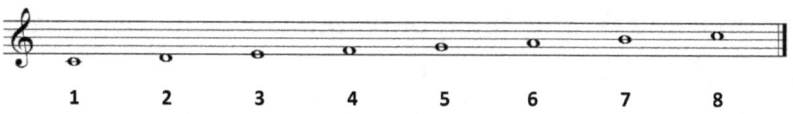

The numbers under the notes of the scale refer to *scale degrees*, which classify the particular functions of the notes within the scale.[3] Thus, in the **C** major scale, **C** is the 1st degree of the scale, **D** is the 2nd degree, **E** is the 3rd degree, etc. When the 8th degree of the scale is reached, it is at the octave of the 1st degree (in this example, **C**).

---

[3] Ibid, p. 41. Cf., *Theory*, p. 60.

Technical names are given to the scale degrees to describe their function within the scale:[4]

1. **Tonic**: the "home tone" or tone of focus of the scale.
2. **Supertonic**: the next tone above the tonic.
2. **Mediant**: the tone halfway between the tonic and its dominant (halfway between 1 and 5).
3. **Sub-Dominant**: the tone a fourth above or a fifth below (the "under dominant") the tonic.
5. **Dominant**: the tone a fifth above the tonic.
6. **Sub-Mediant**: the tone halfway between the sub-dominant and the tonic (halfway between 6 and 8).
7. **Leading Tone**: the tone a *half* step below the tonic, which leads up to it. When it is a *whole* step below the tonic, it is called the **Sub-Tonic**.
8. **Tonic**: the octave of the tonic at scale degree 1.

---

[4]Ibid.

C. KEYS AND KEY SIGNATURES

A *key* is the name given to the tonal center of a scale or musical composition.[5] Thus, the note **C** is the tonal center of the key of **C** major, **G** is the tonal center of the key of **G** major, etc. The designation of the key tells us which note is the tonic, the "home tone", to which all the other notes refer. There are twelve notes in the Western musical system from which keys are formed and scales are built: **A, A# (B♭), B, C, C# (D♭), D, D# (E♭), E, F, F# (G♭), G,** and **G# (A♭)**.

If a musical composition is in the key of **F** major, which has **B♭**, it is much clearer to write this one flat at the beginning of the staff than to write it before each and every **B**. The set of sharps or flats, or the lack of them, at the beginning of a musical line or composition is called a *key signature*.[6]

Example 29

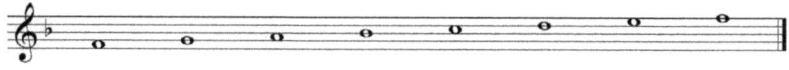

---

[5]*Materials*, p. 34f. Cf., *Theory*, p. 40f.
[6]*Materials*, pp. 42-46. Cf., *Theory*, p. 34f.

Keys and Scales

The key signature gives the music a cleaner look that is easier to read.

The following are the key signatures for all of the flat keys that are major.[7]

Example 30

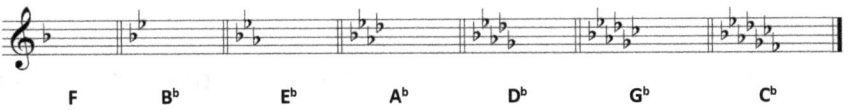

The following are the key signatures for all of the sharp keys that are major.[8]

Example 31

---

[7]*Theory*, p. 35.
[8]Ibid.

The key signature of **C** major has **no** sharps or flats. Since our liturgical music does not use any musical instrument except the human voice, it is unlikely that you will find much of it with key signatures beyond three or four sharps or flats. The complete group of the key signatures is presented here for reference.

D. SOLFEGE SYLLABLES

One of the most widely used systems for reading scale degrees within keys makes use of a series of syllables where one syllable is assigned to each scale degree. These syllables are known as ***solfege syllables***, and the system for using these is called the ***solfege system***.[9] The solfege syllables are **Do**, **Re**, **Mi**, **Fa**, **Sol**, **La**, **Ti**, and (again) **Do**.

There are two variations of the solfege system. One is called the Fixed **Do** System, where a syllable is assigned to each ***note*** (such as **C**, **D**, **E**, etc.). The other one, the Movable **Do** System, assigns a syllable to each ***scale degree*** and, therefore, establishes a ***relationship*** between the solfege syllable and the ***function*** of the scale degree within a given key. This Movable **Do** System is the

---

[9]*Harvard*, pp. 785-786, under "Solfege, solfeggio". Cf., *Theory*, p. 22.

one most prevalent in the United States, and the one that will be presented here.

Play the **C** major scale again on your keyboard, and sing it using the solfege syllables in the example below.

Example 32

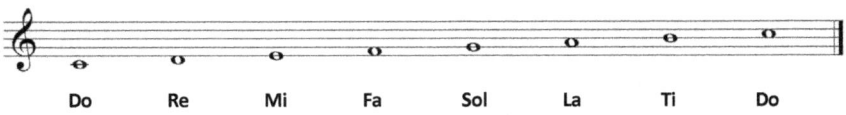

Since there is a half step between **E** and **F**, and again between **B** and **C**, the half steps in the Movable **Do** System *always* fall between the syllables **Mi** and **Fa** and between **Ti** and **Do**. Verify this by singing the solfege syllables in the example below while playing the **F** major scale on your keyboard, playing the black key for B^b.

Example 33

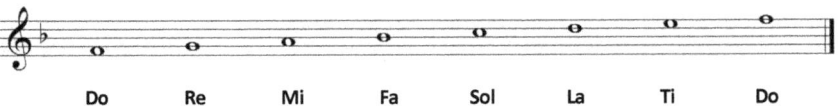

Between **Mi** and **Fa**, there is a half step between **A** and **B**^{b}. There is also a half step between **Ti** and **Do** with the notes **E** to **F**.

E. MINOR KEYS AND SCALES

In the Western harmonic system, keys and scales can be major or minor. One way to remember minor scales is in relation to major scales.[10] Remembering that the tonic is the "home tone" of a key, the tonic of the key of **C** major is the note **C**, which is **Do** in the solfege pattern for a major scale.

Example 34

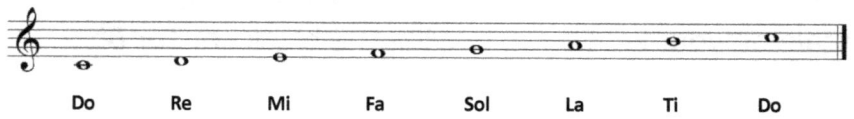

Do   Re   Mi   Fa   Sol   La   Ti   Do

Backing up two notes, a scale can be constructed with no sharps or flats on the note **A**.

---

[10]*Materials*, p. 43.

Example 35

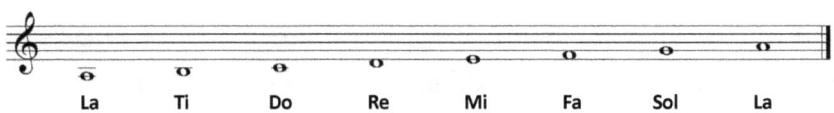

This is an example of a ***minor scale***. When referring to major scales, capital letters are used (***C*** major); minor scales are designated by lower case letters (***a*** minor). Since ***C*** major and ***a*** minor share the same key signature (no sharps or flats), ***a*** minor is the ***relative minor*** of ***C*** major.[11]

The following example illustrates the pattern of whole steps and half steps for a minor scale.

Example 36

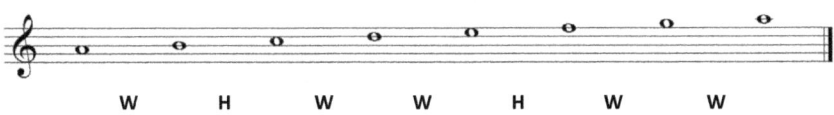

---

[11]Ibid.

Between the "white key" notes of the keyboard there are all whole steps, except between the notes **E** and **F** and the notes **B** and **C**. Thus, as shown in Example 36, the pattern of whole steps and half steps for a ***minor*** scale is: **W**hole, **H**alf, **W**hole, **W**hole, **H**alf, **W**hole, **W**hole, or **W, H, W, W, H, W, W**.[12] Again, it is this particular arrangement of whole steps and half steps which gives this scale the quality of being "minor".

The ***a*** minor scale was constructed by going back two notes from its relative major, **C** major. Therefore, while the tonic or "home tone" of a ***major*** key is ***Do***, the tonic for a ***minor*** key is ***La***. Applying this to all of the minor scales, all minor key signatures can be constructed. The following are the key signatures for all of the flat keys that are minor.[13]

Example 37

d g c f b^b e^b a^b

---

[12]*Theory*, p. 33.
[13]Ibid, p. 35.

Keys and Scales

The following are the key signatures for all of the sharp keys that are minor.[14]

Example 38

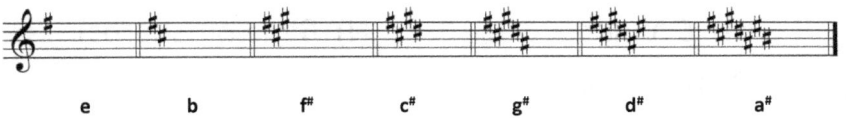

   e   b   f#   c#   g#   d#   a#

Again, occurrences of minor key signatures of more than three or four sharps or flats in our liturgical music will be rare.

The following exercises reinforce the concepts of keys and scales.

EXERCISES • CHAPTER 2

1. Using the pattern of whole steps and half steps for major scales as a guide, construct the following scales. Use the ascending half of the scale only. Any questions as to the use of sharps or flats will be clarified in parentheses.

---

[14]Ibid.

A) **G** major (sharps)
B) **B**^b major
C) **E**^b major
D) **D** major (sharps)
E) **A** major (sharps)
F) **F** major (flats)
G) **E** major (sharps)
H) **F**[#] major
I) **D**^b major
J) **A**^b major
K) **C**[#] major
L) **C**^b major
M) **C** major
N) **B** major (sharps)
O) **G**^b major

2. Using the pattern of whole steps and half steps for minor scales as a guide, construct the following scales. Again, use the ascending half of the scale only.

A) ***d*** minor (flats)
B) ***b*** minor (sharps)
C) ***c*** minor (flats)
D) ***g*** minor (flats)
E) ***e*** minor (sharps)
F) ***f*** minor (flats)
G) ***g***[#] minor (sharps)
H) ***a*** minor
I) ***f***[#] minor
J) ***a***[#] minor
K) ***c***[#] minor
L) ***b***^b minor
M) ***e***^b minor
N) ***d***[#] minor
O) ***a***^b minor

3. Write out the pattern of whole steps and half steps for a major scale.

Keys and Scales

4. Write out the pattern of whole steps and half steps for a minor scale.

5. Write out the key signatures for the following minor scales.

    A) *c* minor   B) *b* minor   C) *d* minor
    D) *e* minor   E) *g* minor   F) *a* minor
    G) *g#* minor   H) *f* minor   I) *a#* minor
    J) *f#* minor   K) *eb* minor   L) *bb* minor
    M) *c#* minor   N) *ab* minor   O) *d#* minor

6. Write out the key signatures for the following major scales.

    A) *A* major   B) *F* major   C) *Eb* major
    D) *G* major   E) *Bb* major   F) *D* major
    G) *C#* major   H) *Ab* major   I) *Db* major
    J) *F#* major   K) *E* major   L) *Gb* major
    M) *B* major   N) *C* major   O) *Cb* major

7. For the following major scales, give the letter name of the note that corresponds to the solfege syllable it that particular key.

    A) *Eb* major: *Do*   B) *G* major: *Sol*
    C) *F* major: *Mi*   D) *A* major: *Ti*
    E) *Bb* major: *La*   F) *Ab* major: *Fa*
    G) *D* major: *Re*   H) *Gb* major: *La*
    I) *B* major: *Do*   J) *E* major: *Ti*

K) $C^\flat$ major: *Mi*
M) $C^\sharp$ major: *Fa*
O) *C* major: *Sol*
Q) *A* major: *Mi*
S) $B^\flat$ major: *La*

L) $F^\sharp$ major: *Sol*
N) $D^\flat$ major: *La*
P) $E^\flat$ major: *Re*
R) *E* major: *Fa*
T) *C* major: *Mi*

8. For the following minor scales, give the letter name of the note that corresponds to the solfege syllable in that particular key.

A) *a* minor: *Re*
C) *e* minor: *La*
E) *b* minor: *Fa*
G) $b^\flat$ minor: *Sol*
I) $f^\sharp$ minor: *Re*
K) $c^\sharp$ minor: *Do*
M) *f* minor: *Fa*
O) $d^\sharp$ minor: *Sol*
Q) $b^\flat$ minor: *Re*
S) *c* minor: *Mi*

B) *g* minor: *Ti*
D) *c* minor: *Do*
F) *g* minor: *Mi*
H) $a^\flat$ minor: *Fa*
J) $g^\sharp$ minor: *La*
L) *d* minor: *Mi*
N) *a* minor: *La*
P) *e* minor: *Ti*
R) $a^\sharp$ minor: *Fa*
T) $a^\flat$ minor: *Sol*

Keys and Scales 51

9. For a major scale, write out the solfege syllables that correspond to the given degree of the scale.

    A) 1st degree   B) 3rd degree
    C) 5th degree   D) 7th degree
    E) 4th degree   F) 2nd degree
    G) 6th degree

10. For a minor scale, write out the solfege syllables that correspond to the given degree of the scale.

    A) 1st degree   B) 6th degree
    C) 3rd degree   D) 5th degree
    E) 7th degree   F) 4th degree
    G) 2nd degree

3
TRIADS

The first two chapters dealt with the horizontal elements of rhythm, pitch, keys, and scales. This chapter focuses on the vertical elements of chords and triads.

A. CHORDS AND TRIADS

Play the *C* major scale on your keyboard, beginning on middle *C*.

Example 39

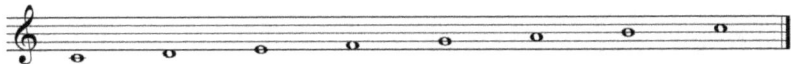

Now play a set of four alternating notes on top of each note of the scale.

Example 40

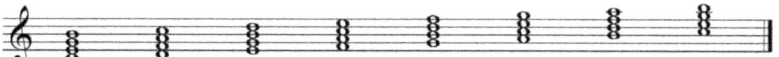

These groupings of notes are called chords. A *chord* is a group of three or more alternate pitches, sounding simultaneously.[1] Building chords of only three alternate pitches on the scale tones results in the following.

Example 41

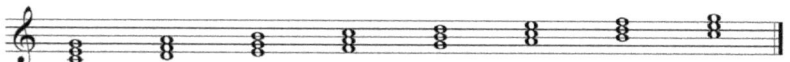

This type of chord is called a triad. A *triad* is a chord of three alternate pitches, consisting of a root, a 3rd, and a 5th.[2] In the first triad of example 41, it begins on middle *C*, skips over *D* to go to *E*, then skips over *F* to go to *G*. The first triad, then, is comprised of

---

[1]*Theory*, p. 49f. Cf., *Materials*, p. 206f.
[2]*Theory*, pp. 52-53. Cf., *Materials*, pp. 28-29.

C, **E**, and **G**. The second triad is made up of **D**, **F**, and **A**; the third triad consists of **E**, **G**, and **B**; etc.

The *root* is the basic tone of a chord or triad.[3] It is the tone on which other chord tones are built. In the first triad above, **C** is the root of the triad. Since **E** is a 3rd above the **C** (**C**, **D**, **E**) and **G** is a 5th above the **C**, **E** is the **3rd** of the triad and **G** is the **5th** of the triad. Looking at the next triad, **D** is the root, **F** is the 3rd, and **A** is the 5th. In the third triad, **E** is the root, **G** is the 3rd, and **B** is the 5th. The same analysis can be made with the remaining triads.

Each note of a scale can be named by a scale degree number. Triads, also, are identified by numbers, most often by Roman numerals.

Example 42

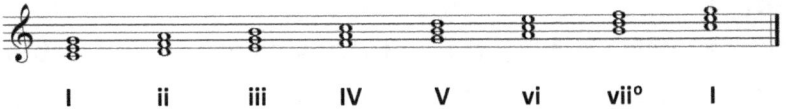

The first triad in this example, made up of **C**, **E**, and **G**, is the first chord in the key of **C** major. Since it is built on the 1st degree of the scale (**C**), it is called

---

[3]*Theory*, p. 50. Cf., *Materials*, p. 25f.

the "I chord" ("one chord") in the key of **C** major. The triad built on the second degree of the **C** major scale (**D**) is called the ii chord; the triad built on the third degree of the **C** major scale (**E**) is called the iii chord; etc.

Play each triad of the **C** major scale again, starting with the I chord. Play up and down the scale on each triad a few times. Become familiar with how the triads differ in quality of sound from each other.

B. QUALITIES OF INTERVALS AND TRIADS

The quality of an interval is determined by how many half steps the top note of the interval is over the bottom note. When abbreviating interval designations, "M" is used for "major", "m" designates "minor", "P" means "perfect", "º" indicates "diminished", and "+" means "augmented".[4] Using these designations, the following example illustrates how many half steps are found in each type of interval within an octave.

---

[4]*Materials*, p. 17.

Example 43

Unison	0 half steps	**m2**	1 half step
M2	2 half steps	**m3**	3 half steps
M3	4 half steps	**P4**	5 half steps
°5 (+4)	6 half steps	**P5**	7 half steps
m6	8 half steps	**M6**	9 half steps
m7	10 half steps	**M7**	11 half steps
octave	12 half steps		

An **augmented interval** is one half step larger than a major or perfect interval, while a **diminished interval** is one half step smaller than a minor or perfect interval; a **perfect interval** refers only to unisons, 4ths, 5ths, and octaves.[5]

Interval sizes can be verified by referring to the illustration of the musical keyboard.

---

[5] Ibid.

Example 44

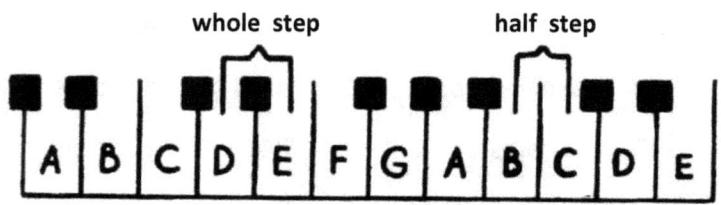

C to *E* is a major 3rd that, according to example 43, is four half steps. The keyboard illustration verifies this, since *C* to *C#* (*D♭*) is one half step, *C#* (*D♭*) to *D* is a second half step, *D* to *D#* (*E♭*) is a third half step, and *D#* (*E♭*) to *E* is the fourth half step. The keyboard can be used to verify all other intervals illustrated in example 43.

How is this information concerning interval sizes useful for our knowledge of triads? It is the combination of various types of intervals that determines the quality of a triad. There are actually three intervals within a triad.[6]

---

[6]*Theory*, p. 53.

Example 45

There is a 3rd from the root of the triad to the 3rd (in this case, *C* to *E*); there is a 3rd from the 3rd of the triad to the 5th (here, *E* to *G*); and there is a 5th from the root of the triad to the 5th (*C* to *G* in this example). Examining the number of half steps involved, it is shown that *C* to *E* is a M3 (major 3rd), *E* to *G* is a m3 (minor 3rd), and *C* to *G* is a P5 (perfect 5th).

Example 46

This is a ***major triad***, which consists of a major 3rd, a minor 3rd, and a perfect 5th.[7] For reference,

---

[7]Ibid.

many major triads that you may encounter are given below.

Example 47

A ***minor triad*** consists of a minor 3rd, a major 3rd, and a perfect 5th.[8]

Example 48

The only difference between major and minor triads is the arrangement of the 3rds. The major triad

---

[8]Ibid.

Triads

has a major 3rd, then a minor 3rd; the minor triad has a minor 3rd, then a major 3rd. Both types of triads have perfect 5ths. For reference, many minor triads that you may encounter are given below.

Example 49

c e♭ g   d f a   e♭ g♭ b♭   e g b   f a♭ c   g b♭ d

a♭ c♭ e♭   a c e   b♭ d♭ f   c# e g#   d♭ f♭ a♭   f# a c#

Another way of looking at qualities of intervals and triads is by examining the relationship between the tones of an interval or triad within the given key of the root note. For example, it can be said that **C** to **E** is a major 3rd because, *in the key of C major*, **E** is natural. Likewise, it can be stated that **C** to **E^b** is a minor 3rd because, *in the key of c minor*, the **E** is flatted (**E^b**). Therefore, a knowledge of key signatures can aid in qualifying intervals and triads.

C. 7ᵀᴴ CHORDS

The triad consists of three alternate pitches, a root, a 3rd, and a 5th. If one more alternate pitch is stacked onto the triad, the result is a 7th chord. A **7th chord** consists of four alternate pitches: a root, a 3rd, a 5th, and a 7th.[9] This last note is called a 7th because it is at the interval of a 7th above the root of the chord.

Example 50

The 7th on top of the 7th chord in this example is **B**^{b}. Since B occurs as **B natural** in the key of **C** major, **C** to **B**^{b} is a minor 7th. This form of the 7th chord, with the minor 7th, is common in music, especially when built on the V chord.

---

[9]*Theory*, pp. 53-55. Cf., *Materials*, p. 313f.

D. INVERSIONS

It is important for choir directors and singers to know what position a triad is in. This has to do with the note in the bass, which is the lowest voice. This bass functions as a foundation for the triad. This foundation is strongest when the root of the triad is in the lowest voice.

Example 51

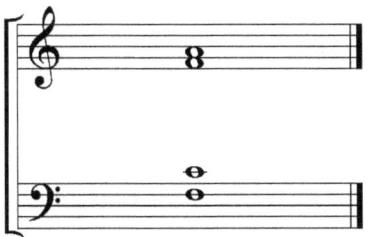

When a triad is built with the root in the lowest voice, the triad is in **root position**.[10] Reading the triad in this example from the bottom up, the **F** major triad has the root on **F** in the bass line, the 5th on **C** in the tenor line, the root on **F** duplicated in the alto line,

---

[10]*Theory*, pp. 52-53. Cf., *Materials*, pp. 224-228.

and the 3rd on **A** in the soprano line. Play this arrangement on your keyboard.

An *inversion* is a redistribution of chord tones out of root position.[11] Replacing the bottom **F** of the triad with **A** will result in the 3rd of the triad being in the lowest voice. Play the following triad arrangement on your keyboard.

Example 52

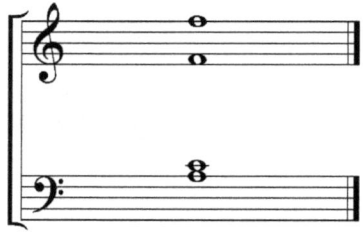

When a triad has the 3rd of the chord in the bass, it is in *first inversion*.

Replacing the **A** in the bass line with the **C** results in the 5th of the triad being in the lowest voice. Play this arrangement of the triad on your keyboard.

---

[11]Ibid.

Example 53

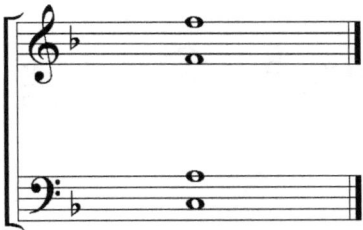

When a triad has the 5th of the chord in the bass, it is in *second inversion*.

The final substitution involves the 7th chord. Play the following arrangement of the 7th chord on your keyboard, with *E^b* in the bass voice, *C* in the tenor, *F* in the alto, and *A* in the soprano.

Example 54

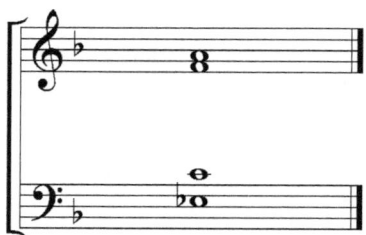

When a 7th chord has the 7th in the bass, it is in ***third inversion***. Play examples 51 through 54 again. Notice that, as the bass note continually gets further away from the root of the chord (first the 3rd, then the 5th, then the 7th), the feeling for the root of the chord becomes weaker.

E. TRIADS IN MAJOR AND MINOR KEYS

The following example illustrates the triads of the key of **C** major. Play these on your keyboard.

Example 55

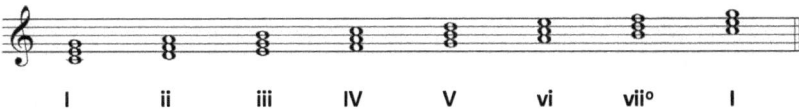

The I, IV, and V chords are represented by capital Roman numerals because they are major triads. The ii, iii, and vi chords are designated by lower case Roman numerals because they are minor triads. The vii° chord is characterized by a lower case Roman numeral with a degree sign because it is a diminished triad, which consists of two minor 3rds and a diminished 5th. An augmented triad consists of two major 3rds and an augmented 5th. This type of triad does not occur naturally in major or minor keys.

The following example illustrates the triads of the key of *a* minor. Play these on your keyboard.

Example 56

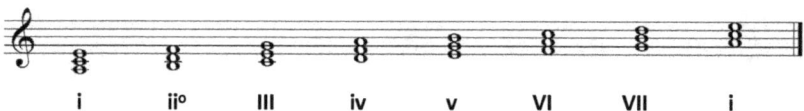

In all but two instances, the triads that were major in the major key are minor here, and vice versa; the ii° chord here is diminished, and the VII chord is major.

F. MUSIC ANALYSIS

This Western system of triadic harmony is prevalent in the music from the Russian and other Slavic traditions. The Byzantine tradition, which utilizes a more linear system of singing in modes, will be discussed later. Play the following example on your keyboard. If possible, gather some singers from your choir, play the initial triad pitches for them, and sing the example.

Example 57

This arrangement of the First Antiphon is a standard one used in choirs utilizing the Russian system of tones. The key signature of one flat indicates that this arrangement is either in the key of **F** major or the key of **d** minor. Since the final chord of this line is an **F** major triad, it is most likely in the key of **F** major.

The basses are on an **F** on "Bless the", tenors are on an **A**, altos are on a **C**, and sopranos are on an **F**. This triad, **F**, **A**, **C**, is the I chord in the key of **F** major. This can be indicated by writing a "I" underneath the bass staff at the word "Bless". On "Lord", there is a 7th chord on the fifth degree of the scale (**C**, **E**, **G**, **B**^{b}). This, then, is a V^7 ("five-seven") chord. On the second half note of the word "Lord", the music returns to a I chord, and stays there until the word "soul". The second quarter note of the word "O" has a **G** in the soprano and a **B**^{b} in the tenor.

Since they do not comprise part of the **F** major triad but are tones that pass between the chord tones, are known as ***passing tones***.[12]

On the word "soul", there is a **B^b** in both the bass and soprano parts, a **D** in the tenor part, and an **F** in the alto part. This is a **B^b** triad (**B^b, D, F**), which is a IV chord in the key of **F** major. With the words "You are", the music returns to a I chord: **F, A, C**. On "blest, O", there is another V^7 chord (**C, E, G, B^b**). On the final word, "Lord", the music ends on a I chord (**F, A, C**) in the key of **F** major. The following example illustrates this again, with the chord designations written beneath the grand staff.

Example 58

---
[12]*Theory*, pp. 171-172. Cf., *Materials*, p. 106.

Triads

The system of writing chord designations beneath the staff is known as *figured bass*.[13]

The following example is of a hymn in a minor key.

Example 59

The key signature and the final chord reveal this to be in the key of *e* minor. The first chord on the "Amen", **B**, **D#**, and **F#**, is a major V chord. As seen in Example 56 above, the v chord is occurs naturally as a minor chord in a minor key. Often, though, the 3rd of

---

[13]*Materials*, p. 226f.

the v chord, which is the seventh degree of the minor scale (in this case, **D**) is raised one half step (here, **D** to **D#**). This is so it will act, not as a subtonic, but as a leading tone to the tonic of the minor key (in this example, **E**).

The second syllable of "Amen" is a i chord on **E**, **G**, and **B**. The phrase "Before Your Cross" alternates the V and the i chords twice. On "we", a VII occurs on **D**, **F#**, and **A**. This is also in effect on "bow", with alto and soprano passing tones on **G** and **B**, respectively. The word "down" embellishes the VII chord to be a VII^7 chord with the strong use of the **C** in the soprano part. Passing tones on the alto **G** and the soprano **B** occur again here. The word "in" returns to a regular VII chord with no 7th. On "wor" of "worship", there is a III chord, **G**, **B**, and **D**. The syllables "ship" and "O" go back to the VII chord, "Mas" is on the i chord, and "ter" returns to the VII chord.

The syllables "and" and "Your" are on the major III chord, "ho" is on the VII chord, and "ly" is on the i chord. With the exception of passing tones, the word "Resurrection" is on the major V chord, (even though the raised 3rd, **D#**, is missing on "rec"), with the prominent 7th, **A**, on "rec". The syllable "glo" of "glorify" has **A**, **C**, **E**, and **G**, a 7th chord built on the fourth degree of the scale, or a iv^7 chord. The syllable "ri" is on a V chord, and the phrase ends with "fy" on the minor i chord.

Triads

The following is the example with its figured bass.

Example 60

Music analysis of this type will not be required of often by Orthodox choir directors and singers. However, becoming familiar with this analysis will assist in deciphering chords in order to give pitches to the choir, which will be discussed in the next chapter. The following exercises reinforce the important concepts of triads and chords presented here.

EXERCISES • CHAPTER 3

1. Given the following keys, construct the chord called for on the treble staff, in root position.

A) *F* major: I chord
B) *e* minor: III chord
C) *C* major: V chord
D) *a* minor: iv chord
E) *d* minor: VI chord
F) *G* major: vii° chord
G) *e*^{b} minor: ii° chord
H) *F*$^\#$ major: V chord
I) *G*^{b} major: vi chord
J) *a*^{b} minor: VII chord
K) *B*^{b} major: iii chord
L) *c*$^\#$ minor: v chord
M) *b* minor: i chord
N) *A* major: vii° chord
O) *a*$^\#$ minor: iv chord
P) *E*^{b} major: ii chord
Q) *B* major: V chord
R) *f* minor: III chord
S) *C*^{b} major: III chord
T) *c* minor: VI chord

2. List all of the intervals used in the following types of triads, from the bottom up.

A) major
B) minor
C) diminished
D) augmented
E) minor 7th chord

3. Explain how to determine if a triad is major.

4. Explain how to determine if a triad is minor.

5. Write out the following triads in first inversion in an SATB (soprano, alto, tenor, bass) setting.

A) *C* major
B) *d* minor
C) *B*^{b} major
D) *e* minor
E) *D* major
F) *g* minor
G) *F*$^\#$ major
H) *a*^{b} minor

I) E^b major J) $a^\#$ minor K) $C^\#$ major L) f minor
M) A major N) $g^\#$ minor O) E major P) b^b minor
Q) C^b major R) e^b minor S) B major T) a minor

6. Write out the following triads in second inversion in an SATB setting.

A) a minor B) F major C) g minor D) G major
E) b minor F) $C^\#$ major G) e minor H) A^b major
I) d minor J) B major K) a^b minor L) D major
M) $c^\#$ minor N) B^b major O) f minor P) G^b major
Q) c minor R) E major S) e^b minor T) C^b major

7. Write out the following 7th chords in third inversion in an SATB setting. Use a minor 7th in the chords from the root.

A) A major B) c minor C) E^b major D) $f^\#$ minor
E) E major F) b minor G) A^b major H) $a^\#$ minor
I) G major J) $g^\#$ minor K) $C^\#$ major L) f minor
M) $F^\#$ major N) $d^\#$ minor O) D major P) b^b minor
Q) F major R) e minor S) D^b major T) a^b minor

8. Explain how to get to a relative minor key from a major key.

9. Write out the Roman numerals for the naturally occurring chords of a major key.

10. Write out the Roman numerals for the naturally occurring chords of a minor key.

4
GIVING PITCHES

The ability to efficiently and accurately give pitches to a choir is one of the most important skills that a choir director will need to master. The correct singing of the liturgical hymns; the liturgical flow of the services; the confidence of the choir director in himself or herself; the confidence of the choir in the choir director; all of these factors are directly dependent on the important ability of the choir director to give pitches.

Before giving the pitches, the choir director must be aware of where each section of the choir is positioned. There are different "floor plans" that are used by various choirs to position their sections. The following example illustrates one of the most commonly used positionings for an SATB (soprano, alto, tenor, bass) choir.

Example 61

	Altos	Sopranos	
Basses			**Tenors**
	Choir Director		

This placement of the sections follows the pattern of a piano keyboard, with higher-pitched voices on the right and lower-pitched voices on the left. It is important to note that the choir director should face the singers when directing, and not the priest or the sanctuary. During longer prayers, such as the Anaphora, the choir director may then face the sanctuary and focus on the prayer being read.

Another item of importance for giving pitches is the tuning fork. The tuning fork is a necessary tool, especially for beginning choir directors, precisely because it provides a point of **reference** for the chord to be given. The stress here is on the reference, because singing a hymn in the key in which it is written is not a hard-and-fast rule. Other factors may enter into which key the hymn will be pitched in: the note that the priest, deacon or bishop is on; how many singers (and in which sections) are present for the given service; the weather (damp, rainy weather puts an added strain on the vocal cords); and the physical condition of the singers themselves (some may have colds or sore throats). Many experienced choir directors, after years of using the tuning fork and having a good tonal memory for the reference pitch, are able to effectively abandon the use of the tuning fork and give the pitches from memory. The standard tuning fork used by most Orthodox choir directors in parishes utilizing music in the Western triadic system is the one pitched on **C** at 573.3 vibrations per second. The tuning fork pitched on **A** at 440 vibrations per second can be used as a supplementary tool.

A. TRIADS

The Movable **Do** System of solfege singing as outlined in the previous chapter can be quite useful in giving pitches to a choir.

Example 62

This example illustrates a chord frequently found at the beginning of Orthodox hymns using the Western triadic system of harmony. The key signature of **B**♭ tells us that this hymn is either in the key of *F* major or in the key of *d* minor. The basses have an **F**, the tenors are on a **C**, the altos also chord, we have **F, A, C**, or an **F** major triad. There is a good chance, then, that this hymn is in the key of **F** major.

It is customary to give the triad in descending order; that is, first give the **C** to the tenors, then give the **A** to the sopranos, and then give the **F** to both the altos and the basses. The reason for this is that, by ending on the root of the chord, a feel for the triad is reinforced. Using the Movable **Do** solfege syllables, the choir director could sing the **C** on the syllable "**Sol**", the **A** on "**Mi**", and the **F** on "**Do**".

Example 63

The key signature of one sharp in this example indicates a key of either **G** major or **e** minor. The basses have a **G**, the tenors are on **D**, the altos come in on **G**, and the sopranos are singing a **B**. The notes of this chord, **G**, **B**, **D**, form a **G** major triad. The solfege syllables used to give this chord in descending order would be **Sol**, **Mi**, **Do**. Play Example 62, with its **F** major triad, without singing it; then, again without singing, play the **G** major triad as given in Example 63. Do this a few times, first by playing the notes successively as you would give them to the sections of the choir (tenors, sopranos, altos and basses), and then by playing the notes of each chord simultaneously. Notice the similarity in sound quality between the two triads. This is what makes the Movable **Do** System so valuable, because it associates the sound quality and patterns with the syllables. Once you become familiar with how a major triad sounds on the syllables *Sol*, *Mi*, *Do*, you will be able to select any note, and from that note sing a major triad by just using the syllables *Sol*, *Mi*, *Do*.

The Movable *Do* syllables can be useful in moving to a different key from the reference tone of the tuning fork. For example, to give the **G** major triad in Example 63 from a **C** tuning fork, you could play the note **C** on the tuning fork and call it *Do*; then, by singing "*Do*, *Re*" in your mind, you would reach the note **D** on the syllable *Re*. Renaming the note **D** as the syllable *Sol*, you would then sing the pitches of a **G** major triad (**D**, **B**, **G**) on the syllables *Sol*, *Mi*, *Do*.

Example 64

Another common voicing for the major triad is given below.

Example 65

Here, the 5th of the triad, **C**, is in the alto and the 3rd, **A**, is in the tenor, with the root, **F**, in both the soprano and the bass. One way to give this pitch is to sing down the chord in your mind to the root on **F**. Give this note to the sopranos, then go up to the tenors for the **A**. Since the sopranos do not normally have their note in the beginning chord, come back to them and give them their **F** again for reinforcement. Go down to the **C** for the altos, and back up to the **F** for the basses. The following, with the notes in parentheses being the ones you "sing" in your mind, would be the order of pitches given: (**C, A,**) **F, A, F, C, F**. Another way to give this set of pitches is to start with the **F** for the sopranos, go up to the **A** for the tenors, ***back to the F*** for the sopranos, down to the **C** for the altos, and then up to **F** for the basses. The order of pitches in this pattern, then, is: **F, A, (F), C, F**.

The following example illustrates some major triads in voicings as you would commonly find them in our Orthodox hymnography.

Example 66

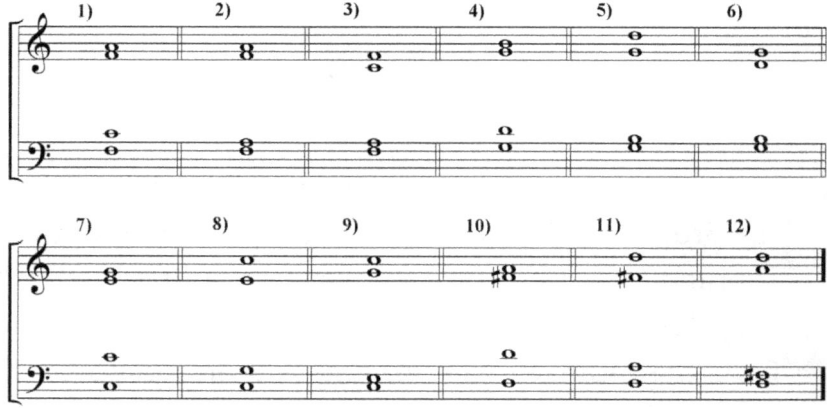

Items 1 through 3 are in the key of *F* major, items 4 through 6 are in the key of *G* major, items 7 through 9 are in the key of *C* major, and items 10 through 12 are in the key of *D* major. Practice singing these examples using the Movable *Do* solfege syllables, then check yourself by playing them on your keyboard. Remember to sing the parts in the following order: tenor, soprano, alto, and bass.

The following example illustrates some minor triads in voicings as you would commonly find them in our Orthodox hymnography.

Example 67

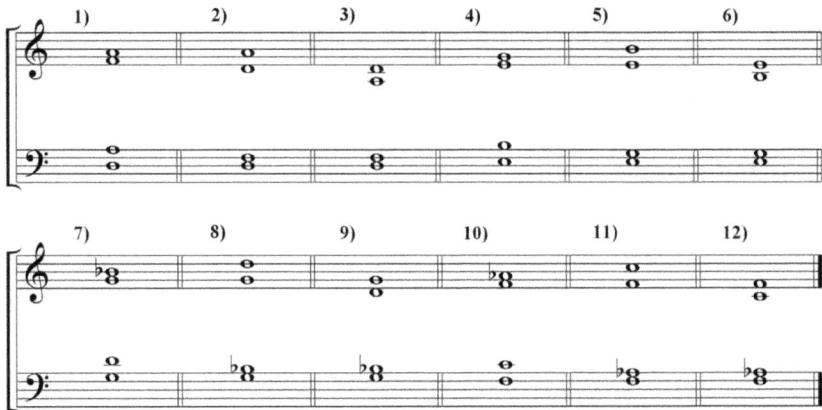

Items 1 through 3 are in the key of *d* minor; items 4 through 6 are in the key of *e* minor; items 7 through 9 are in the key of *g* minor; and items 10 through 12 are in the key of *f* minor. Again, practice giving these pitches off of a *C* tuning fork, then double-check them on your keyboard.

B. INVERSIONS

Chords in first, second, or third inversion are not as common in Orthodox hymnography as those found in root position. However, since they do sometimes occur, it is useful for the choir director to be able to easily recognize these chords and effectively give the pitches to the singers.

Example 68

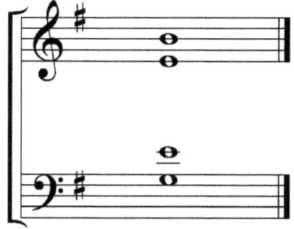

The key signature of one sharp indicates either *G* major or *e* minor. The bass has a *G*, the tenor has an *E*, the alto also has an *E*, and the soprano has a *B*. Rearranging these chord tones into root position, there is *E*, *G*, *B*, an *e* minor triad, with the 3rd, *G*, in the bass. Since this is the key of *e* minor, the solfege syllables in descending order will *not* be *Sol*, *Mi*, *Do*,

Giving Pitches

but will be **Mi**, **Do**, **La**. Giving the pitches from tenor to soprano to alto to bass (with the parenthetical syllables representing those pitches to be sung in your mind), it would be **La**, **Mi**, (**Do**,) **La**, **Mi**. It would be advisable to end by repeating the root of the chord, **E**, on the syllable **La** for the altos, to reinforce the minor **e** triad.

C. 7TH CHORDS

Giving pitches for 7th chords will most likely occur for the previously discussed V^7 chord. Again, this chord consists of a major triad with a minor 7th added on.

Example 69

Here, the key is **F** major. The V⁷ chord is made up of the notes **C**, **E**, **G**, and **B**ᵇ. Many times, the 3rd on **E** is omitted in order to double up on the root of the chord, **C**. Since **C** is the 5th degree of the **F** major scale, it will have the solfege syllable **Sol**. Giving the pitches in descending order for this chord would encompass the following: **Sol**, **Fa**, **Re**, **Sol**. In the hymnography of the Russian tradition, this is the initial chord for stikhera tones 1 and 5, and for the tradition lenten litany melody.

EXERCISES • CHAPTER 4

The best ongoing exercise for giving pitches is to practice with as many hymns as possible, first identifying the key and corresponding initial chord (V chord in the key of **F** major, i chord in the key of *e* minor, etc.), working out the chord tones with the Movable **Do** solfege syllables, getting to the chord from the **C** on the tuning fork, singing the chord, and then comparing this with the chord as you play it on your keyboard. The more you practice, the sooner you will become proficient at giving pitches.

Giving Pitches

Utilize the following examples to practice giving pitches. After you try each one, check out how accurate you were by playing the selection on a keyboard.

5
MELODY AND HARMONY

Melody is the horizontal set of pitches organized in time that determines the shape of a musical line.[1] As such, melody incorporates elements of both pitch and rhythm.

A. MOTIVES AND PHRASES

A ***motive*** is the smallest distinctive melodic germ, made up of a few tones and rhythms.[2] A ***phrase*** is a complete musical idea that ends with a cadence.[3] A ***cadence*** is a musical ending or closing section.[4] A motive, therefore, provides the melodic kernel of a phrase.

---

[1]*Theory*, p. 101.
[2]Ibid, p. 102.
[3]Ibid.
[4]*Materials*, p. 53f. See also *Theory*, p. 86f.

Example 70

The motive in this example, taken from an arrangement of the Cherubic Hymn by Gregory Lvovsky, is distinctive both in pitch and in rhythm. The rhythmic element consists of a dotted quarter note, followed by an eighth note, and then two quarter notes. A **dot** increases the value of a note or rest by one half.[5] Pitchwise, there is a **G**, followed by an **A**, then back to **G**, and descending to **F#**. The shape of the motive forms an arch or curve, ascending and descending. The shape of a motive or phrase is called its **contour**.[6] This contour, combined with the specific rhythmic pattern, gives this motive its unique character and makes it recognizable, even when it occurs later in the hymn at a different pitch level.

---

[5]*Theory*, p. 13.
[6]*Materials*, p. 71f.

Example 71

Here, the motive begins on an **A** rather than a **G**. However, it still retains its basic rhythmic pattern and melodic contour.

B. ANTECEDENT – CONSEQUENT PHRASES

There are patterns of phrases, which occur commonly in Orthodox liturgical music, which share a question-and-answer relationship with each other. Such phrases are called **antecedent-consequent phrases**.[7] They form an "A-B" type pattern, whereby the first, antecedent phrase is countered by the consequent phrase.

---

[7]*Materials*, p. 75. See also *Theory*, p. 104.

Example 72

This example is a tone 3 setting for "Lord, I Call Upon You" from the Common Chant tones of the Russian tradition. The first phrase can stand by itself. Musically, however, there is a feeling of incompleteness, a feeling that the music needs to be resolved to a complete ending. This is accomplished in the second phrase, where the cadence on "Lord" gives the feeling of resolution and "answers" the first phrase.

C. MONOPHONY

Harmony is the chordal or vertical structure of a musical composition.[8] Whereas melody is constructed horizontally with the elements of pitch and rhythm, harmony uses intervals, triads, and chords as its basic tools. There are a variety of

---

[8]*Harvard*, p. 371, under "Harmony".

harmonic textures that is found in Orthodox liturgical music.

Monophony is music consisting of a single melodic line without additional parts or accompaniment.[9]

Example 73

There is a lack of vertical harmony or intervals in this example. The simple, horizontal melody makes it easy to teach to children, and also aids in prayerful concentration on the words of the hymn.

---

[9]Ibid, p. 539, under "Monophony, monophonic".

D. DIOPHONY

Diophony is music consisting of a single melodic line with a second line that is not melodic.[10] Diophonic music often makes use of an ***ison***, a repeated tone which functions as a reference pitch for the melody.[11]

Example 74

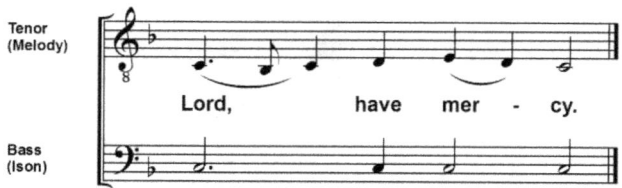

---

[10]Many music theory textbooks loosely categorize this harmonic texture as "monophonic". However, it is ***not*** strict monophony. Because of its historic prevalence in Byzantine chant, this harmonic texture can be aptly called "diophonic", a term first coined by Dr. Vladimir Morosan.

[11]Wellecz, Egon, *Byzantine Music and Hymnography*, 2nd Edition, Oxford at the Clarendon Press, Oxford, England, 1980 (hereafter referred to as "*Byzantine*"), p. 16.

The symbol below the treble clef, **8** (which could also be rendered ***8va-***), indicates that the tenor part is sung an octave lower than written. This eliminates the need for ledger lines. The tenor has the melody, as indicated. The ison in the bass part, on the note **C**, does not function as accompaniment in the Western sense of harmonic chords, but serves as a point of reference for the melody, which is focused on the note **C**. This example of Byzantine chant, then, is not in the "key" of **C** (major or minor). However, since the focus of the melody and the ison does center around this note, this example is in the **modality** of **C**, making using of the Byzantine system of modes.

E. HOMOPHONY

Homophony is music consisting of a single melodic line with harmonic accompaniment.[12] Most Orthodox liturgical music that uses the Western triadic system of harmony is homophonic.

---

[12]*Harvard*, p. 390, under "Homophony". See also *Materials*, p. 116f.

Example 75

The melody in this example is in the soprano. The tenor has a harmonization of the melody, up a 3rd. The contour of this harmonization parallels that of the melody. The alto and bass parts are filling in chord tones. Homophonic music is the easiest texture to analyze chord progressions using figured bass.

F. POLYPHONY

Polyphony is a musical texture consisting of two or more independent melodies or lines.[13] It can

---

[13]*Harvard*, p. 687, under "Polyphony". See also *Materials*, p. 116f.

be the use of two different melodies, or the use of the same melody sung by different voices at different times.

Example 76

Here, the sopranos and altos share the same basic melody, but at different times and at different pitch levels. The soprano part is centered around the note **B**, while the alto part is centered around the note **G**. Because of its more complex structure, which can tend to distract from liturgical prayer and worship, the polyphonic texture is used with restraint in Orthodox liturgical music.

EXERCISES • CHAPTER 5

The best exercises you can do in relation to the concepts discussed in this chapter are to apply them throughout your years as a choir director. Each time you are going to direct or rehearse a hymn, become familiar with the melodic elements of pitch and rhythm found within the motives, the melodic kernels that make up the melody. See where the musical phrases occur, and if there is any relationship between them, such as found with antecedent-consequent phrases. Identify the type of harmonic texture the hymn is composed in, whether it be monophonic, diophonic, homophonic, or polyphonic. As you gradually integrate these various elements into your experience, you will bring the musical expression of the hymn forward and manifest the beauty of our Orthodox liturgical hymnography.

6

BYZANTINE CHANT

A. ESSENCE OF CHANT

Chant is defined as "a repetitive liturgical melody in which as many syllables are assigned to each tone as required".[1] Chant, then, involves the use of a singing voice.   However, the aspects of conversational speech are not totally discarded. This type of speaking is known as *prose*.[2] In the early Church, *prose texts* were set to *prose rhythms*, either through reading (i.e., using a monotonic recitation of the texts with cadences) or through chanting melodies which followed the natural curve of prose sentences, keeping their free, unmetered form.[3] This is what was referred to earlier as *free meter*, which is organized, not according to a set of fixed beats per minute (as in strict meter), but according to the rhythmic patterns inherent *in the text*. Free meter, then, is actually text

---

[1] Merriam-Webster, A., *Webster's Seventh New Collegiate Dictionary*, G. & C. Merriam Company, Springfield, MA, 1970 (hereafter referred to as "*Webster's*"), p. 139.
[2] Ibid, p. 684.
[3] Douglas, Winfred, *Church Music in History and Practice*, Charles Scribner's Sons, New York, NY, 1937 (hereafter referred to as "*Church Music*"), p. 28.

meter, and the irregular amount of beats between the accentuations of the text determines the rhythm of the chant melodies.

Some confusion results in the use of the term "chanting". Some use it to mean only the reading of texts in a monotone with inflections of the voice at the cadences; others term it to mean using free, unmetered melodies. Here, the former will be referred to as "reading" (as in reading the Epistle or the Hours at a Divine Liturgy), and the latter will be referred to as "chanting".

The setting of prose **texts** to prose **rhythms** means that the natural accentuation of the text is retained in the chant itself.

Example 77

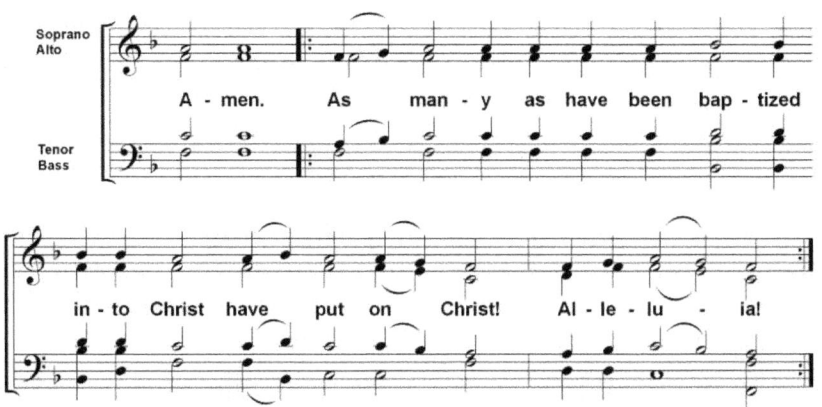

Read the text of this hymn aloud in conversational speech (prose), paying special attention to where the accents in the text occur. The textual accentuations fall on the syllables "man" (in "many"), "bap" (in "baptized"), "Christ", "put", the second word "Christ", and "lu" (in "Alleluia"). Looking at the example, the music brings this accentuation out naturally, in the use of both melodic contour (shape of the phrase) and longer note values (half notes, instead of quarter notes). Therefore, the prose **rhythm** of the prose **text** is brought out in the musical elements. A 9th century definition that differentiates the terms "meter" and "rhythm" states that "meter is melody in mathematical measure, while rhythm is melody without mathematical measure, determined by the number of syllables".[4] This use of prose rhythms in music is the most characteristic quality of the Christian chant.[5]

B. BYZANTINE CHANT AND OKTOECHOS

Byzantine chant is vocal, as are the other forms of Orthodox liturgical music. Early on, it was monophonic, whether sung by one singer or by a choir.[6] What has been referred to here as "monophonic", music composed and performed in a single melodic line, Egon Wellecz calls "homophonic".[7] The importance here lies not in the technical terminology, but in the actual musical texture used by the Byzantines in their chant. It **was** originally monophonic in the strict sense of that term; at a later stage, the ison developed.[8]

The important feature of the Byzantine chant is the use of the **Oktoechos**, or "Eight Tones", where "tones" refers to the "echoi" or "modes" that are the

---

[4]Ibid, p. 21.
[5]Ibid, p. 19.
[6]*Byzantine*, p. 32.
[7]Ibid, p. 32 n.
[8]Ibid, pp. 253, 269.

pattern melodies.[9] The melodies of each tone consist of a number of formulae, or melodic "kernels", which make up the particular pattern of the tone, rather than a scale. The task of the composer was to adapt these melodic kernels to the texts of the hymns to enhance the syntax of the phrases.[10]

To establish the "feeling" of the tone or mode to be used, a pattern of notes called the ***intonation formulae*** were used.[11] These formulae had two functions. If they came between verses, they served to link the recitation of the preceding verse with the verse that followed it. If no verse preceded it (which, in its present usage, is most often the case), it functioned as a **preparation** or **announcement** of the tone (mode) of the melody.[12] This is similar to the function of giving pitches for chords in music of the Western harmonic system.

The intonation formulae model the Fixed **Do** System, using a Greek syllable for each note of a particular letter name.

---

[9] Ibid, p. 71.
[10] Ibid.
[11] Ibid, pp. 303-309. See also Lungu, N.; Costea, G.; and Croitoru, I., *A Guide to the Music of the Eastern Orthodox Church*, trans. Nicholas K. Apostola, Holy Cross Orthodox Press, Brookline, MA, 1984 (hereafter referred to as "*Guide*"), p. 58f.
[12] *Byzantine*, p. 305.

Example 78

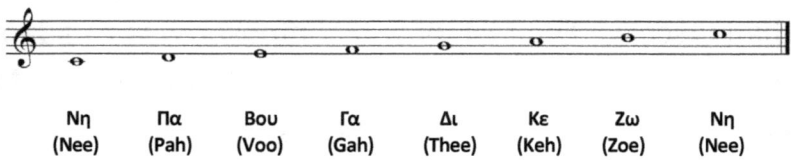

The following example illustrates the various intonation formulae for the eight Byzantine tones.

Example 79

Tone 1

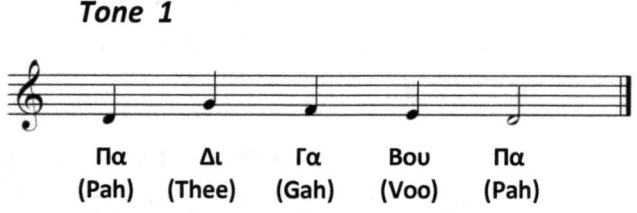

Tone 2

Byzantine Chant

Tone 3

Γα	Δι	Κε	Δι	Γα	Βου	Γα
(Gah)	(Thee)	(Keh)	(Thee)	(Gah)	(Voo)	(Gah)

Tone 4

Βου	Γα	Δι	Κε	Δι	Γα	Βου
(Voo)	(Gah)	(Thee)	(Keh)	(Thee)	(Gah)	(Voo)

Tone 5

Κε	Ζω	Νη	Ζω	Κε
(Keh)	(Zoe)	(Nee)	(Zoe)	(Keh)

Tone 6

Δι	Κε	Ζω	Κε	Δι	Γα	Δι
(Thee)	(Keh)	(Zoe)	(Keh)	(Thee)	(Gah)	(Thee)

Tone 7

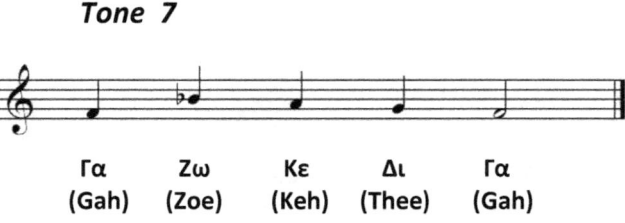

Γα	Ζω	Κε	Δι	Γα
(Gah)	(Zoe)	(Keh)	(Thee)	(Gah)

Tone 8

Νη	Βου	Δι	Βου	Νη
(Nee)	(Voo)	(Thee)	(Voo)	(Nee)

Tones 5 through 8 are called "plagal" because they are derived from or related to tones 1 through 4.[13] Therefore, tone 5 is plagal 1 (related to tone 1), tone 6 is plagal 2, tone 7 is plagal 3, and tone 8 is plagal 4. Tone 7, in addition to being plagal 3, is also called **Varys**, meaning "grave", because of the somber quality of its melody.[14]

The ison of a melody can be distinguished in one of two ways. One way is to show just the melody with the letter name of the designated ison note

---

[13] *Guide*, p. 48.
[14] *Byzantine*, p. 303.

above the staff. The other way is to write out the notes for both the melody and the ison. Example 80, which follows, shows both ways.

Example 80

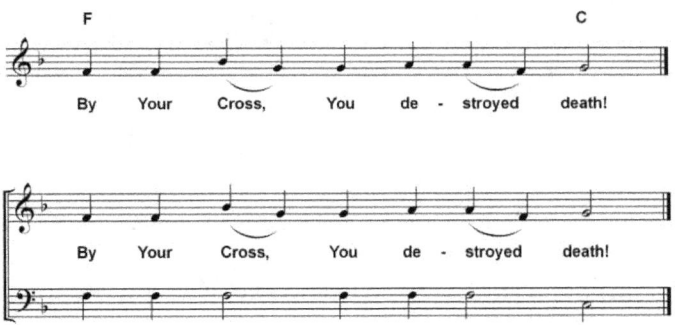

The following examples contain one melody and accompanying ison each for Byzantine chant tones 1 through 8.

Example 81

Tone 1

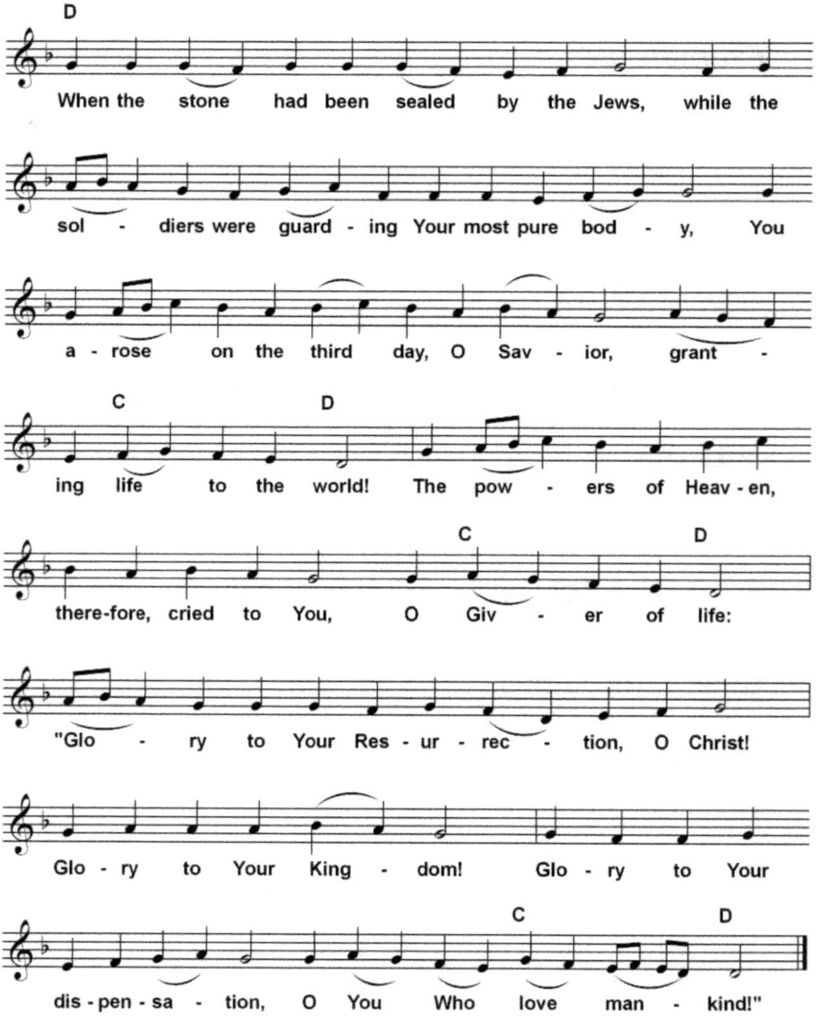
D
When the stone had been sealed by the Jews, while the
sol - diers were guard - ing Your most pure bod - y, You
a - rose on the third day, O Sav - ior, grant -
C D
ing life to the world! The pow - ers of Heav - en,
C D
there-fore, cried to You, O Giv - er of life:
"Glo - ry to Your Res - ur - rec - tion, O Christ!
Glo - ry to Your King - dom! Glo - ry to Your
C D
dis - pen - sa - tion, O You Who love man - kind!"

Example 82

Example 83

Example 84

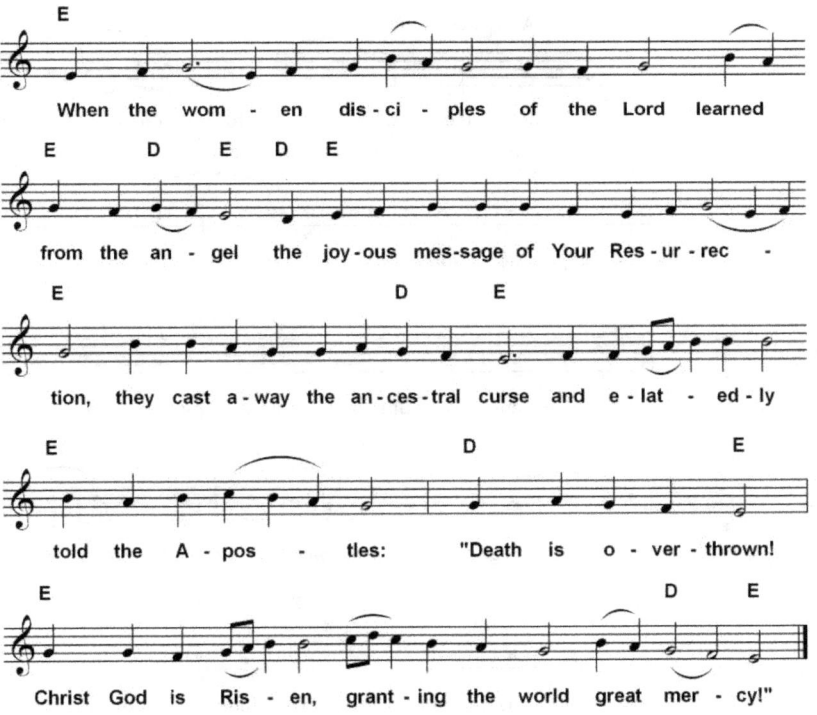

Example 85

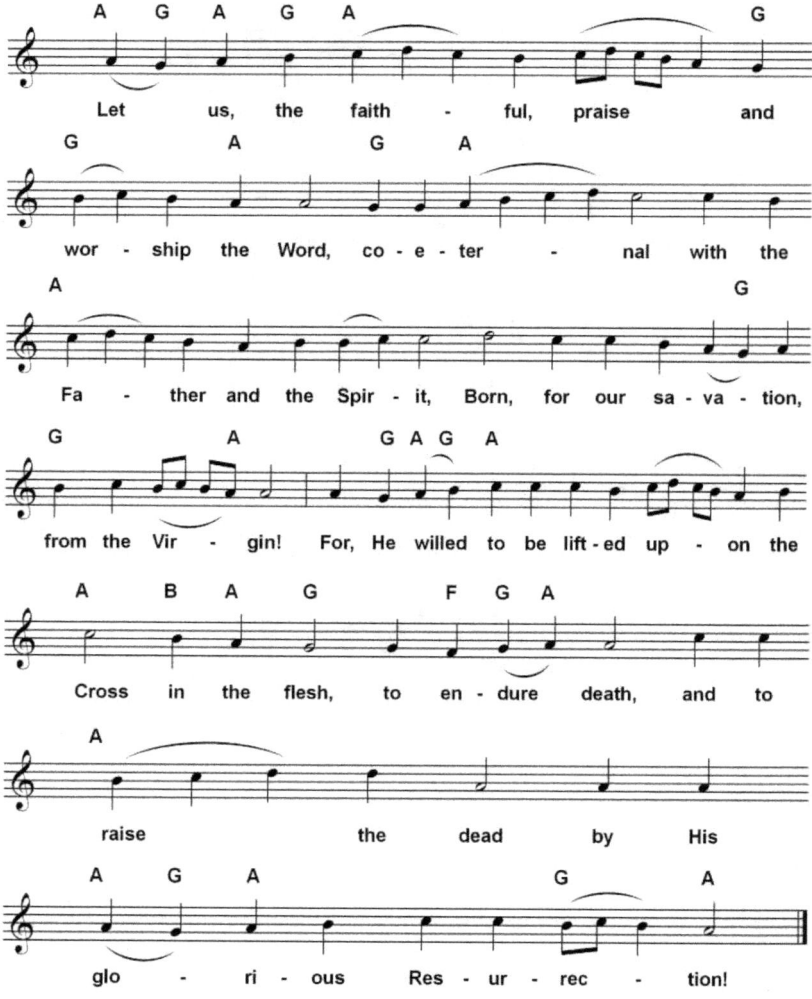

Example 86

Tone 6

Example 87

Example 88

Tone 8

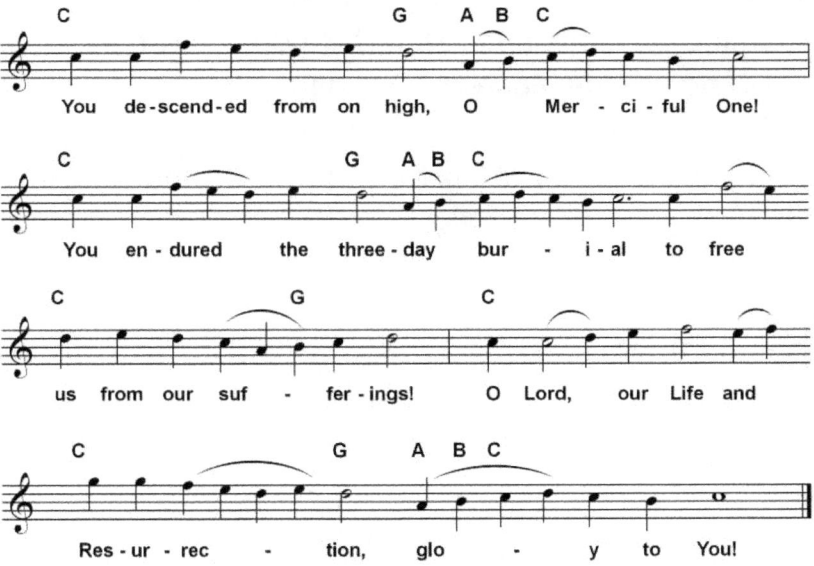

EXERCISES • CHAPTER 6

The best exercises for the materials presented in this chapter are to sing hymns set in the Byzantine chant system of tones. The book, **A Guide to the Music of the Eastern Orthodox Church**, by Lungu, Costea, and Croitoru, is an excellent and thorough analysis and workbook for learning Byzantine chant.

7
RUSSIAN CHANT

The Russian chant system differs from the Byzantine tradition in that it employs the use of the Western system of triadic harmony.[1] This is the system of major and minor keys and scales discussed earlier. The Russian chant makes use of a system called **Obikhod**, or "Common Chant", and its present usage is an abbreviated form of Kievan chant.[2] The Russian Oktoechos differs in structure and pattern melodies from those of the Byzantine tradition. Many tonal systems of the countries of Eastern Europe (Serbian, Romanian, etc.) are derived from or similar to the tones of the Russian chant system. The Oktoechos of the Russian tradition is further divided into four groupings of eight tones: stikhera tones, troparion tones, prokeimenon tones, and kanon tones. These four groupings will be presented here, followed by the stikhera tones of the Kievan Chant

---

[1]von Gardner, Johann, *Russian Church Singing: Orthodox Worship and Hymnography, Volume 1*, trans. Vladimir Morosan, St Vladimir's Seminary (SVS) Press, Crestwood, NY, 1980 (hereafter referred to as "*Russian*"), p. 63f, especially p. 64, n. 67. What Gardner refers to as "polyphony" is the musical texture we called "homophony", that is, a single melodic line with harmonic accompaniment.

[2]Ibid, p. 58f, especially p. 58, n. 59.

system, the use of which is being revived in some parishes today.

A. STIKHERA TONES

Stikhera tones are the tones used for the ***stikhera*** (verses) of such liturgical propers as "Lord, I Call Upon You" and the Apostikha in Vespers.[3] A "***proper***" is a liturgical element that changes, depending on the specific tone of the week or specific feast being celebrated. An "***ordinary***" is a liturgical element that remains constant within the service, such as The Lord's Prayer.

The melody for each stikhera tone in the Russian Oktoechos is in the alto part.

---

[3] Ibid, pp. 35-37.

Example 89

Stikhera tone 1 has four pattern phrases, ending with a cadence phrase (designated as "C"). After singing pattern phrase 4, the pattern resumes again with pattern phrase 1. The order of pattern phrases for stikhera tone 1, then, is 1, 2, 3, 4, 1, 2, 3, 4, etc., C.

The initial chord for stikhera tone 1 is a V^7 chord in the key of **F** major, with the third of the chord, **E**, omitted.

The note within the solid lines of each phrase is known as the **recitative**, or reciting tone, where many syllables are sung on the same note.[4] The note within the dotted lines at the beginning of pattern phrases 1

---

[4]*Harvard*, p. 718, under "Recitative, I.".

and 3 is a pick-up, which is used if the text for these phrases begins on an unaccented syllable.

The four-part SATB (Soprano, Alto, Tenor, Bass) setting for stikhera tone 1 is as follows.

Example 90

Stikhera tone 2 has four pattern phrases and a cadence phrase.

Example 91

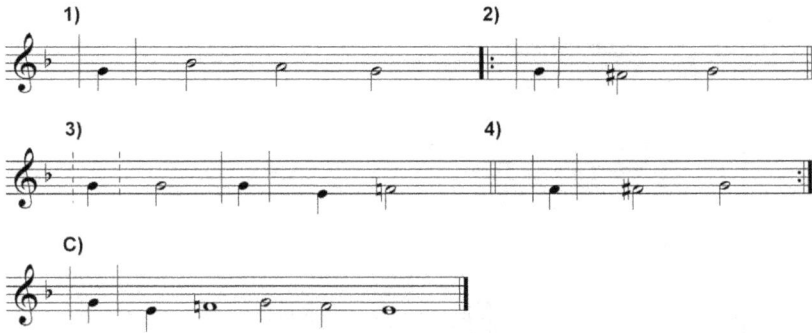

In this tone, pattern phrase 1 is sung only once, at the beginning of the stikheron. After singing pattern phrase 4, the tone returns to pattern phrase 2 to repeat the pattern. Therefore, the order of phrases for stikhera tone 2 is 1, 2, 3, 4, *2, 3, 4, 2, 3, 4*, etc., C.

The key signature of one flat seems to suggest the key of **F** major. However, the emphasis on **G**, with the corresponding use of the raised **F** to **F**# as a leading tone to **G**, suggests a modulation to **g** minor. A **modulation** is the process of changing the key or tonic.[5]   Stikhera tone 2, then, begins on a *g* minor triad.

Example 92

---

[5]*Theory*, p. 94. See also *Materials*, p. 47.

Russian Chant

The order of pattern phrases for tone 3 is 1, 2, etc., C.

Example 93

The tone is in a major key, here, the key of **G** major.

Example 94

Stikhera tone 4 has six pattern phrases, followed by a cadence phrase. After pattern phrase 6, the pattern returns to pattern phrase 4. The order of pattern phrases, then, is 1, 2, 3, 4, 5, 6, 4, 5, 6, 4, 5, 6, etc., C.

Example 95

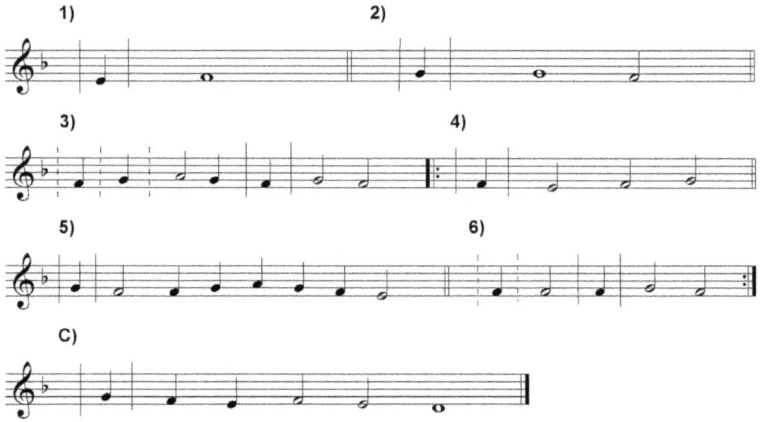

The one flat in the key signature, along with the melody, indicates the key of **F** major. The initial chord is a major V^7 chord, given in descending order: **C, G, E, C**.

In phrase pattern 3, there are two quarter note pick-ups shown. If there is only one pick-up note (such as in the phrase, "The Lord"), the second pick-up note, on **G**, will be used. If there are two pick-up notes (such as in the phrase, "When the Lord"), both pick-up notes, the one on **F** and the one on **G**, will be used.

Example 96

Stikhera tone 5's pattern phrases are 1, 2, 3, etc., C.

Example 97

As with tone 1, tone 5 begins on a V^7 chord in **F** major.

Example 98

Stikhera tone 6 is minor, with three pattern phrases. If pattern phrase 2 comes just before the cadence, however, a special version of pattern phrase 2 (2*) is used.

Example 99

Example 100

Stikhera tone 7 has two pattern phrases and a cadence phrase. If it begins accented, the chord is a V^7 chord in the key of *F* major. If it begins unaccented, the chord is a I chord.

Example 101

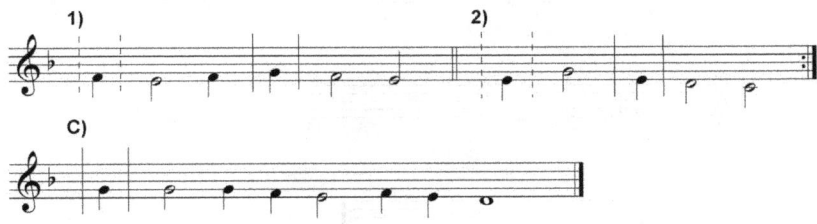

Example 102

Stikhera tone 8's pattern phrases are 1, 2, 3, 4, 2, 3, 4, 2, 3, 4, etc., C.

Example 103

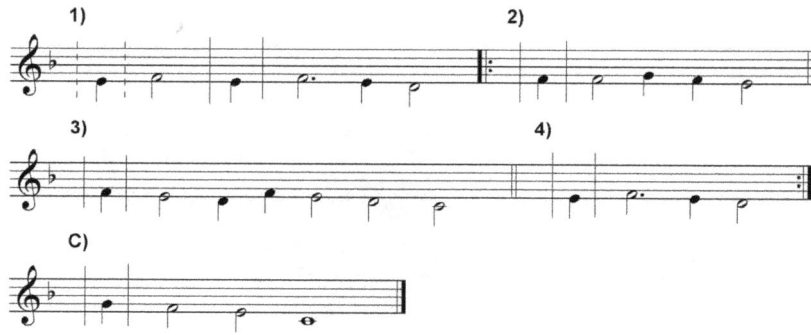

The chord for this tone is the opposite arrangement that it was for stikhera tone 7. If the hymn text begins on an accented syllable, the I chord in the key of **F** major (**C, A, F**) is given in descending order. If the text begins on an unaccented syllable, the V chord (**C, G, E, C**) is used.

Example 104

B. TROPARION TONES

Troparion tones are the tone patterns used for singing the troparion and the kontakion of a feast day.[6]   With the exception of the melodies for troparion tone 4 and troparion tone 5, all of the melodies for the troparion tones are in the soprano part.

Troparion tone 1 has two pattern phrases, followed by a cadence phrase. Some parishes also use phrase pattern 1 as the cadence phrase.

Example 105

---

[6]Ibid, pp. 38-39.

If the tone begins on an accented syllable, the triad is a V chord in the key of **F** major. It frequently begins, on an unaccented syllable, with the use of a I chord. The order of pitches, however, differs slightly from the standard arrangement. Here, the altos have the *C* and the tenors have the **A**. The director can either give the pitches in descending order; or he or she can first give the **F** to the sopranos, then **A** for the tenors, and down the chord again for the remaining parts: **F**, **A**, (**F**), **C**, **F**.

Also, phrase pattern 2 should **never** come right before the cadence phrase. If the setting is such that this phrase pattern **would**, in the normal course of the setting, come right before the cadence phrase, then the bridge phrase replaces phrase pattern 2 in this instance.

Example 106

Troparion tone 2 has two pattern phrases and a cadence phrase.

Example 107

Beginning accented, it is found on the I chord in the key of **F** major. Beginning unaccented, the V chord is used.

Example 108

Troparion tone 3 contains four pattern phrases and a cadence phrase. However, unlike the other tones, there is no specific order for the pattern other than beginning on pattern phrase 1 and ending with the cadence phrase. The determining factor in the order of the pattern phrases is how many **textual** phrases comprise the specific troparion or kontakion being sung. The cadence phrase can be preceded by any of the four pattern phrases.

Example 109

Any of three chords can be used to begin the tone. If the specific troparion or kontakion begins on an accented syllable, a I chord in the key of **F** major is used, with the same voicing as found at the unaccented beginning of troparion tone 1. If it begins on **one** unaccented syllable (which is rarely found), a V^7 chord is used. If the hymn begins on **two or more** unaccented syllables, a minor vi chord is used, with again the same voicing as the unaccented beginning of troparion tone 1, the difference being that this vi chord is minor, rather than major.

Example 110

The adapted melody for troparion tone 4 has the melody in the alto part, with two pattern phrases and a cadence phrase. The pitch for this tone is a I chord in the key of **F** major.

Example 111

With only a few altos, it is preferable in phrase pattern 2 and the cadence phrase to take the **E**, rather than the **G**. This is because the 3rd of the chord is more important than the 5th, which can be eliminated, if necessary.

Example 112

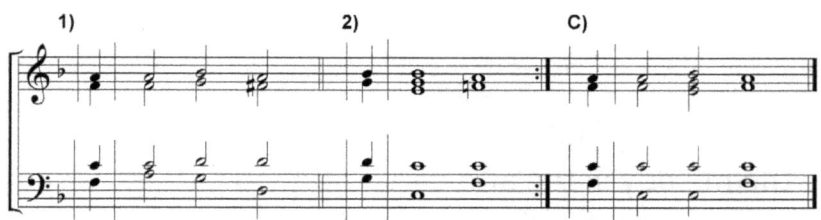

Troparion tone 5 is the only tone that is almost the same as its corresponding stikhera tone. Whereas with stikhera tone 5, the setting is on a 7th chord, troparion tone 5 is built on a regular **C** chord.

Example 113

Example 114

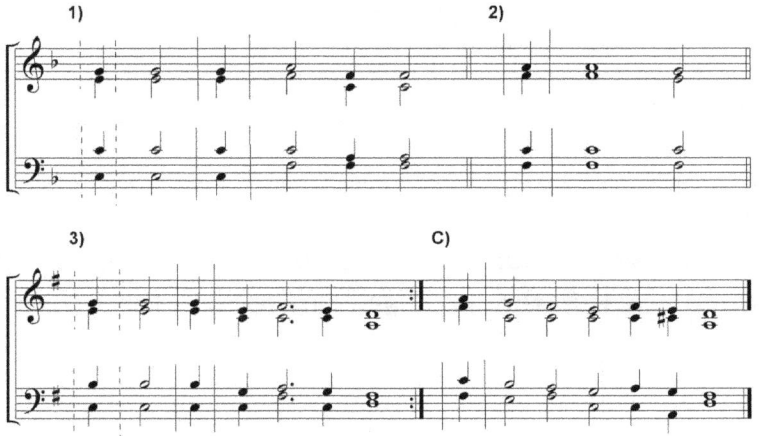

Troparion tone 6 has two pattern phrases, with the second also serving as the cadence phrase.

Example 115

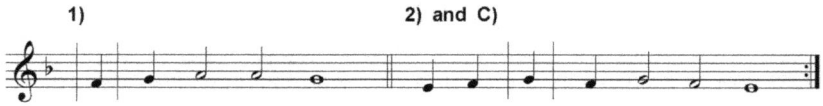

The initial chord is an **F** major triad.

Example 116

However, some parishes using a voicing where the melody is in the alto part, rather than the soprano part.

Example 117

Troparion tone 7 has two pattern phrases and a cadence phrase.

Example 118

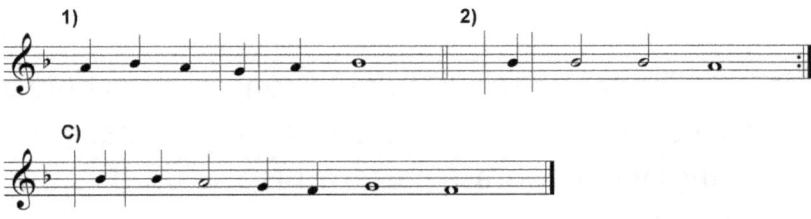

Unlike some other tones, the notes before the recitative in pattern phrase 1 are not pick-up notes, but part of the tone pattern. The tone begins on a I chord in the key of **F** major, then, whether the text begins accented or unaccented.

Example 119

Troparion tone 8 has only one pattern phrase and a cadence phrase. However, many parishes use settings where phrase pattern 1 is also used as the cadence phrase.

Russian Chant

Example 120

The pitch is the same voicing for the *F* major triad as found for the unaccented beginning of troparion tone 1.

Example 121

However, as with troparion tone 6, many parishes using a voicing where the melody is in the alto part, rather than the soprano part.

Example 122

C. PROKEIMENON TONES

Prokeimenon tones are the tones used to sing the prokeimenon in Vespers, the Divine Liturgy, and, at times, Matins.[7] Unlike the other tones, prokeimenon tones do not consist of various pattern phrases followed by a cadence phrase. It is one pattern, subdivided in the middle at the point where

---

[7]Ibid, pp. 49-50.

the reader, on reading the prokeimenon verse for the last time, will the first half of the verse, and the choir or people respond with the last half of the verse. In the examples that follow, this breaking point will be denoted by a double bar line.

Prokeimenon tone 1 has the melody in the alto part.

Example 123

The pitch for this tone is an **F** major triad.

Example 124

The melody for prokeimenon tone 2 is found in the soprano part.

Example 125

It begins on a **g** minor triad, with **B**^{b} in the tenor and **D** in the alto.

Example 126

Prokeimenon tone 3 has the melody in the soprano part.

Example 127

It begins on an **F** major triad.

Example 128

Prokeimenon tone 4 also has the melody in the soprano part.

Example 129

The initial chord is an **F** major triad.

Example 130

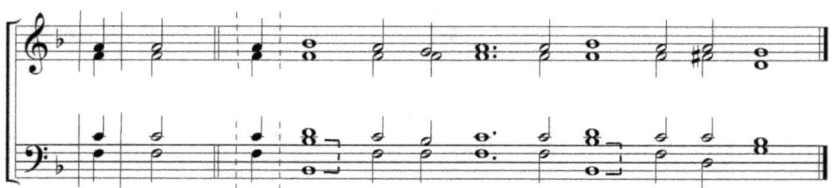

Prokeimenon tone 5 has the melody in the alto part.

Example 131

It begins on a **g** minor triad.

Example 132

The melody for prokeimenon tone 6 is in the alto part.

Example 133

It also begins on a *g* minor triad.

Example 134

Prokeimenon tone 7's melody is in the alto part, and the first half is the same as phrase pattern 1 of stikhera tone 7. The second half is *similar* to the cadence phrase of stikhera tone 7, but not exactly the same.

Example 135

The pitch for this tone is on an **F** major triad.

Example 136

Prokeimenon tone 8 has its melody in the soprano part.

Example 137

The beginning chord is a *g* minor triad.

Example 138

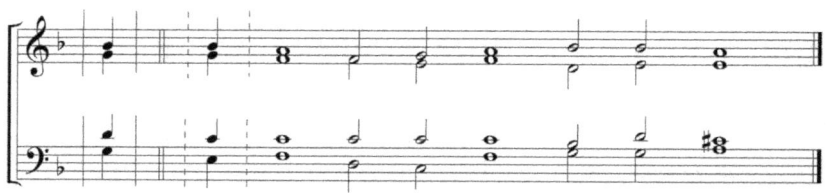

D. KANON TONES

Kanon tones are the tone patterns sung for the **irmi** (**heirmi**) on the odes of the kanon in Matins.[8] Like the stikhera and troparion tones, kanon tones have pattern phrases and cadence phrases. With the exception of kanon tones 3 and 4 (where the melody is in the soprano part), the rest of the kanon tones have the melody in the alto part.

---

[8] Ibid, pp. 40-44.

Russian Chant

Kanon tone 1 has two pattern phrases plus a cadence phrase. The order of pattern phrases, then, is 1, 2, 1, 2, etc., C.

Example 139

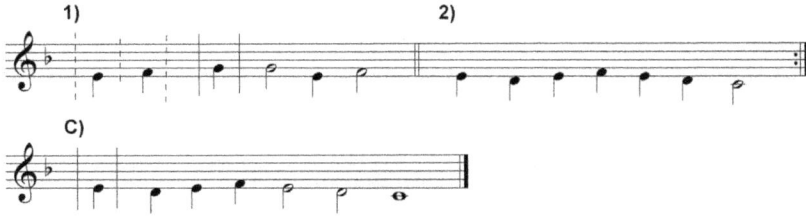

The pitch for this is either a V^7 chord in the key of **F** major, a I chord with the 5th repeated in the bass (**C, A, F, C**), or a regular V chord, depending on where the accents fall at the beginning of the hymn text.

Example 140

The order of pattern phrases for kanon tone 2 is 1, 2, 3, 1, 2, 3, etc., C.

Example 141

If the hymn text for this tone begins on an accented syllable, the pitch is a major VII^7 chord in the key of *d* minor (*C, B^b, G, C*). If the hymn text begins on an unaccented syllable, the pitch is a minor i chord (*a, f, d*).

Example 142

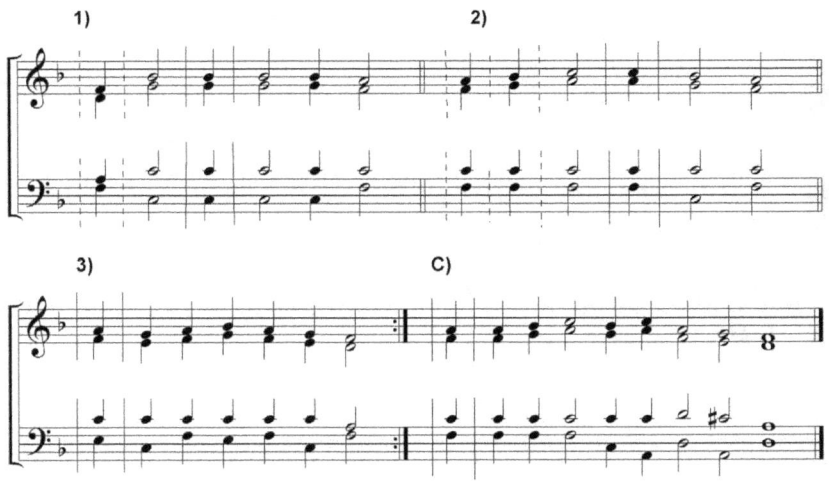

The order of pattern phrases for kanon tone 2 is 1, 2, 3, 1, 2, 3, etc., C.

Example 143

If the hymn text for this tone begins on an accented syllable, the pitch is a major VII^7 chord in the key of **d** minor (**C, B^b, G, C**). If the hymn text begins on an unaccented syllable, the pitch is a minor i chord (**a, f, d**).

Example 144

If the text for kanon tone 3 begins on an accented syllable, the pitch is a I chord in the key of **F** major, with the tenors taking the 3rd on **A** and the altos taking the 5th on **C**. If the text begins on **one** unaccented syllable (which rarely occurs), the pitch is a V^7 chord, with the 5th in the tenors (**G**), the 3rd in the sopranos (**E**), the 7th in the altos (**B**^{b}), and the root in the bass (**C**). If the text begins on **two or more** unaccented syllables, the pitch is a minor vii chord (***a***, ***f***, ***d***), with the 3rd in the tenors and the 5th in the altos.

Example 145

Kanon tone 4 has two pattern phrases plus a cadence phrase. The order of pattern phrases, then, is 1, 2, 1, 2, etc., C. Like kanon tone 3, it has the melody in the soprano part.

Russian Chant

Example 146

The pitch is a major chord on **D**: **D**, **A**, **F**#, **D**.

Example 147

Kanon tone 5 has four pattern phrases and a cadence phrase. The order of pattern phrases is 1, 2, 3, 4, etc., C.

Example 148

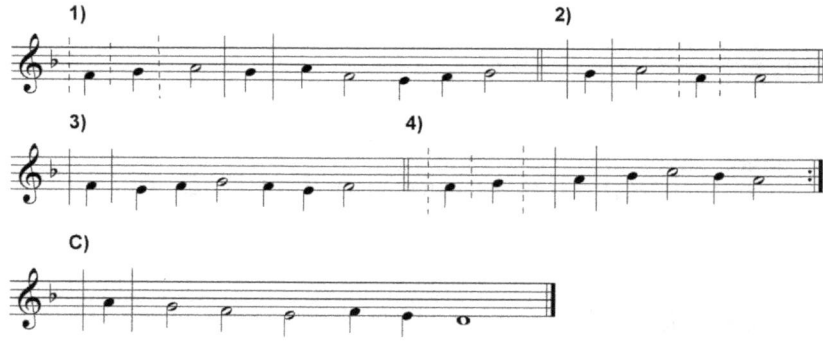

If the hymn text for this tone begins on an accented syllable *or* two or more unaccented syllables, the pitch is a major III chord in the key of *d* minor (*C, A, F*). If it begins on just one unaccented syllable, the initial chord is a VII^7 chord, minus the 3rd (*C, B^b, G, C*).

Example 149

Kanon tone 6 contains four pattern phrases and a cadence phrase. After pattern phrase 4, the music returns to pattern phrase 2. The order, then, is 1, 2, 3, 4, *2*, 3, 4, etc., C.

Example 150

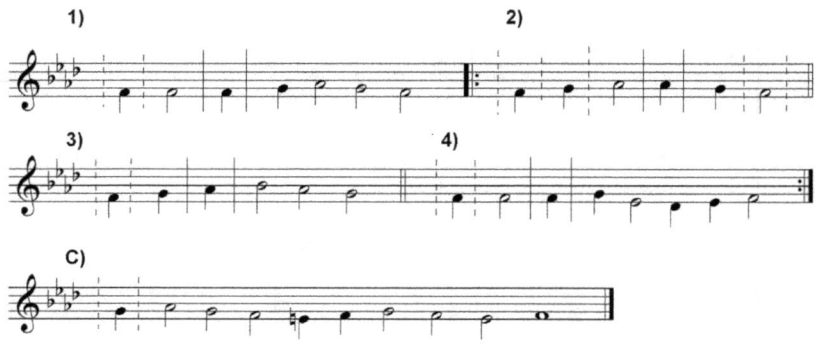

Whether the hymn text begins on an accented or an unaccented syllable, the initial pitch is a i chord in the key of *f* minor (*c*, *a*^{b}, *f*).

Example 151

Kanon tone 7 has four pattern phrases and a cadence phrase. Since the music returns to pattern phrase 3 after pattern phrase 4, the order is 1, 2, 3, 4, 3, 4, 3, 4, etc., C.

Example 152

With an accented hymn text beginning, the initial triad is a V chord in the key of **F** major (**C, G, E, C**). If the beginning of the text is unaccented, a I chord is used (**C, A, F**).

Be careful not to confuse this kanon tone 7 with stikhera tone 7. Pattern phrase 1 is the same for **both** tones. However, beginning with pattern phrase 2, each tone moves in a different melodic direction.

Example 153

The order of pattern phrases for kanon tone 8 is 1, 2, 1, 2, etc., C.

Example 154

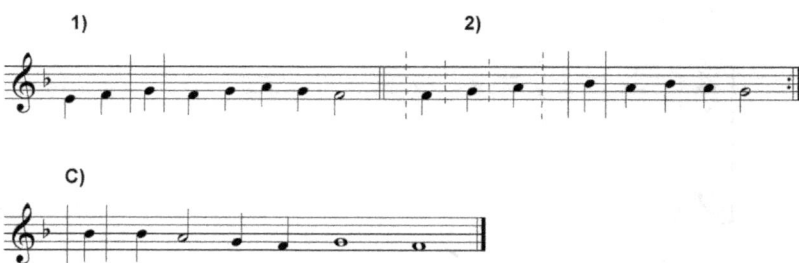

The pitch for this tone is a V chord in the key of F major (**C, G, E, C**).

Example 155

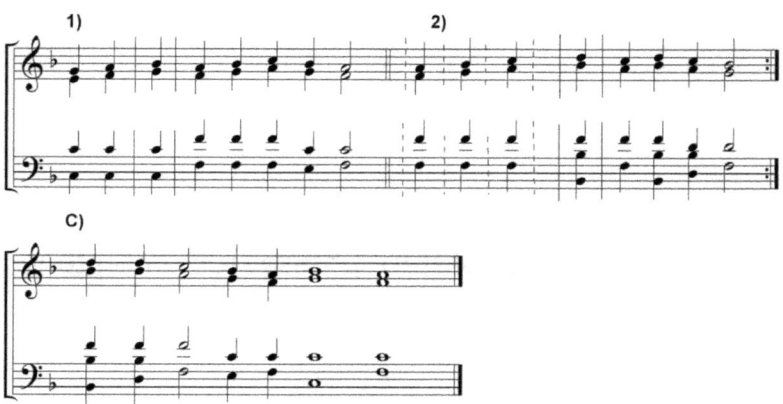

E. KIEVAN CHANT STIKHERA TONES

As previously mentioned, the Russian **Obikhod** ("Common Chant") stikhera tones are "watered down" or simplified settings of the Kievan Chant stikhera tones. These more elaborate Kievan Chant tones are becoming increasingly more utilized in parishes for singing the stikhera at Vespers. For this reason, a brief presentation of these Kievan Chant stikhera tones is given here.

Unlike the more simplified Russian tones, the Kievan Chant stikhera tones do not have the melody in the alto line but in the soprano part.

The following is the melody, in the soprano line, for Kievan Chant stikhera tone 1. It consists of four phrase patterns and a cadence phrase.

Example 156

As with the other tones, the notes within the dotted brackets in phrase patterns 1 and 3 are for unaccented words or syllables acting as pick-up notes, and the notes within the solid brackets in phrase patterns 1 through 4 are for the recitative.

The pitch for this tone is a V chord (**D**, **A**, **F#**, **D**) in the key of **G** major.

Example 157

Tone 2 consists of five phrase patterns and a cadence phrase. If there are multiple stikhera and the pattern needs to be repeated, after phrase pattern 5 the melody returns to phrase pattern 3. Thus, the set of phrase patterns for this tone is 1, 2, 3, 4, 5, 3, 4, 5, 3, 4, 5, etc., C.

Example 158

The pitch for this tone is a V chord (*D*, *A*, *F*#, *D*) in the key of *G* major.

Example 159

Tone 3 has two phrase patterns and a cadence phrase.

Example 160

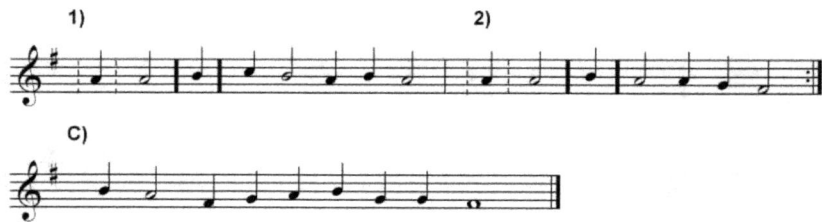

The pitch for this tone is a V chord (**D**, **A**, **F#**, **D**) in the key of **G** major.

Example 161

Tone 4 has six phrase patterns and a cadence. With multiple textual phrases, the phrase patterns go from the sixth phrase pattern back to the fourth one and forward, as many times as needed. Therefore, the phrase patterns are 1, 2, 3, 4, 5, 6, 4, 5, 6, 4, 5, 6, etc., C.

Example 162

The pitch for this tone is a V chord in the key of **G** major (**A**, **F#**, **D**), with the **A** in the tenor, the **F#** in the soprano, and the **D** doubled in both the alto and the bass.

Example 163

Tone 5 consists of three phrase patterns and a cadence phrase.

Example 164

The pitch for this tone is a V chord (**D**, **A**, **F**#, **D**) in the key of **G** major.

Example 165

Tone 6 consists of three phrase patterns and a cadence phrase.

Example 166

Russian Chant

The pitch for this tone is a iv chord (*e*, *c*, *a*) in the key of *a* minor. The best way to give this pitch is to take the **C** right from the **C** tuning fork, giving this note (*c*) to the tenors as ***Do***, going down to the *a* for the sopranos as ***La***, going down again to *e* for the altos as ***Mi***, and back up to the *a* for the basses as ***La***. Therefore, the order of pitches is ***Do, La, Mi, La***.

Example 167

Tone 7 consists of four phrase patterns and a cadence phrase.

Example 168

A word of explanation for phrase pattern 2: If this happens to fall on a very short phrase that starts on an accented word or syllable (such as, "**Hear** me, O Lord!"), this accented word or syllable will fall on the half note on **D**. Otherwise, the phrase will begin on the quarter note on **D**, continue on through the passing tone on **C**, and on to the recitative on **B**.

The pitch for this tone is a IV chord (**C, E, G**) in the key of **G** major. The best way to give this pitch is to begin with the **C** for the sopranos on **Fa**, up to the **E** for the tenors on **La**, **back down** to the **C** for the sopranos (again on **Fa**), down to the **G** for the altos on **Do**, and down further to the **C** for the basses on **Fa**. Therefore, the pattern is **Fa, La, [Fa], Do, Fa**.

Example 169

Tone 8 is made up of three phrase patterns and a cadence phrase.

Example 170

The pitch for this tone is the same as for the previous one, tone 7: a IV chord (*C*, *E*, *G*) in the key of *G* major. The best way to give this pitch is to begin with the *C* for the sopranos on *Fa*, up to the *E* for the tenors on *La*, **back down** to the *C* for the sopranos (again on *Fa*), down to the *G* for the altos on *Do*, and down further to the *C* for the basses on *Fa*. Therefore, the pattern is *Fa, La, [Fa], Do, Fa*.

Example 171

EXERCISES • CHAPTER 7

The best exercises to do to master these tone groups are to study and practice the melodies and harmonizations of each of the tones, then practice them in settings of stikhera, troparia and kontakia, prokeimena, and kanon irmi. When you become very familiar with each tone, practice singing each voicing of the tone (soprano, alto, tenor, and bass) to the liturgical texts without music.

8
CONDUCTING AND REHEARSING

The abilities to effectively conduct a choir during the liturgical services and efficiently run a choir rehearsal are basic skills that a choir director needs to master. Conducting a choir involves familiarity with the conducting plane and the beat patterns used in the conducting of the hymnography.

The **conducting plane** is the area in space in which the conductor moves his or her hands.[1] The vertical portion of the plane extends from the crown of the head to about waist level. The horizontal part covers the area between the perimeters of the arms as they hang naturally by the side of the body. This is shown in the example on the following page.

---

[1] Rudolf, Max, *The Grammar of Conducting*, 2nd Edition, Schirmer Books, Macmillan Publishing Company, Inc, New York, NY, 1980 (hereafter referred to as "*Grammar*"), pp. xviii and 1.

Example 172

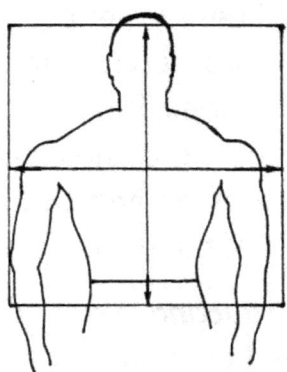

A. BEAT PATTERNS

There are three basic beat patterns that are used most frequently in the conducting of our hymnography.[2] One of these, the 4-pattern, utilizes all four directions of the conducting plane: ***down***, ***left***, ***right***, ***up***.

---

[2] Ibid, pp. 1-10, 35-43, and 61-67.

Example 173

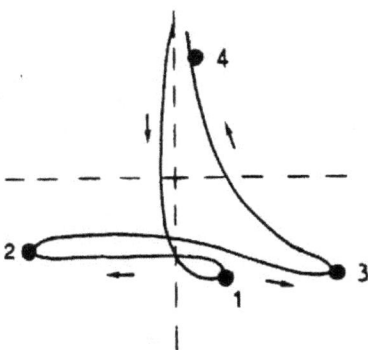

Notice that the graph illustrates a conducting style that involves a smooth change of direction from one beat to another. Although some music may, at times, call for an abrupt, snappy moving of the hands, this style in general is more appropriate for instrumental music. The vocal character of our Orthodox hymnography calls for a smoother style of hand movement.

Hand position is very important in determining a comfortable, relaxed style of conducting. Generally, the hand should be held in front of the body, palm down, with the fingers kept close together but not pressing into each other. All movement should be at the wrist, not in the elbow or upper arm.

Example 174

The important thing to remember in developing a comfortable hand position is to hold it naturally and relax. Tension and unnatural positioning of the hands leads to many conducting problems.

Another basic beat pattern is the 2-pattern. It resembles a backwards letter "J". The downward movement ends at the right side of the waist, and the upward movement culminates at the crown of the head. The directions for the 2-pattern, then, are: ***down, up.***

Example 175

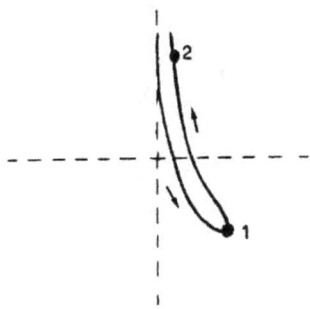

The 3-pattern begins moving in the opposite direction than the 4-pattern did. After the downbeat, the 4-pattern moved to the left. The 3-pattern moves to the right after the downbeat, and then finishes with an upward movement to the crown of the head. The directions for a 3-pattern are: **down, right, up**.

Example 176

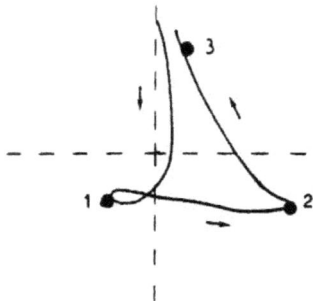

These three basic beat patterns should be comfortably mastered before applying them to any conducting style.

B. CHANT STYLE

The strict, metered style of conducting, in which each measure contains the same number of beats, is found and used the least in our Orthodox hymnography. The two conducting styles utilized the most for our liturgical music are the chant style and the stikhera style.

The **chant style** of conducting uses combinations of different meters that are organized according to the *text*.[3] In other words, it is the way the **accents of the text** occur that determines where musical downbeats will occur and, therefore, what combination of meter patterns will be used.

Primary textual accents, then, must occur on the downbeats. In singing the initial "Amen" of any service, for example, the downbeat must be on the syllable "men", since this is where the accent of the word is found. Using the four possible directions of conducting (down, left, right, and up), the first syllable of the "Amen" should be directed with a beat going up. Before singing that first syllable, however, the choir must be prepared to sing by directing a beat which will both show them the speed at which they will be singing and give them an opportunity to take a breath beforehand. This beat is called the **preparation beat**.[4] Using arrows to determine the direction of the conductor's hands, the following

---

[3]Lamb, Gordon H., *Choral Techniques*, William C. Brown Company, Dubuque, IA, 1976, p. 141.
[4]*Grammar*, pp. 4-5.

example illustrates how the "Amen" is to be conducted.

Example 177

The arrow within the parentheses symbolizes the preparation beat, on which nothing is sung. By moving on the preparation beat to the right, the hand is then in the natural position to move up on the first syllable of "Amen", and then come down for a downbeat on the second, accented syllable.

If the first syllable to be sung was accented, as in the word "Glory", the preparation beat would be going up, so as to have a downbeat on the accented syllable.

Example 178

$$(\rightarrow) \quad \downarrow$$

Glo - ry

To direct the entrance of a hymn, then, it is important to find where the initial downbeat will occur (on the first accented syllable), and then **back up** in the sequence of beat patterns (down, up, right, left) until coming to the preparation beat.

The following example illustrates a hymn that can be examined in applying the chant style of conducting.

Example 179

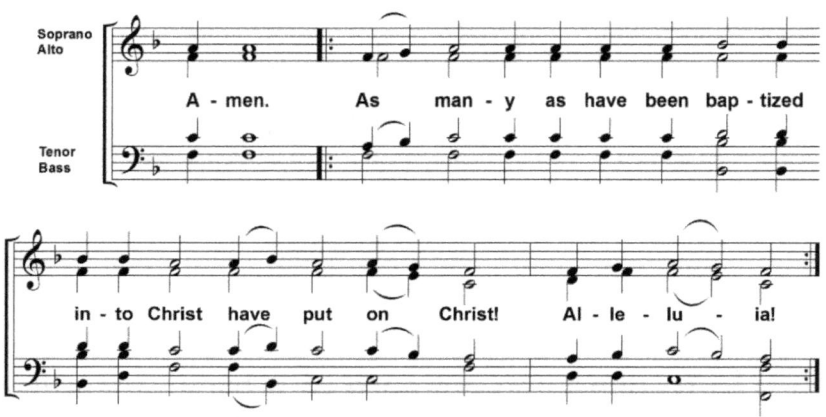

Saying the text out loud, primary accents can be found on the following syllables: the second syllable of "Amen"; the first syllable of "many"; the first syllable of "baptized"; "Christ"; "put"; the second word "Christ"; the third syllable of "Alleluia". To direct this with a beat on each quarter note would make it plodding and heavy. Using the half note as the basic beat would render the singing of this hymn much smoother. Many hymns in the chant style use the half note as the basic beat.

Conducting and Rehearsing

The quarter note at the beginning of the word "Amen" comes in on the second half of a half note beat. To give a preparation beat on only the first half of a beat, the drop preparation beat is used. This consists in holding your hand straight out in front of you, at mid chest level, and dropping the wrist and forearm to waist level. When the hand starts moving **up** from the waist back to the crown of the head, this is where the second half of the beat occurs and where the singing begins. On the second syllable of "Amen", a 1-beat should be used. This is done by dropping the hand from forehead to waist and back to forehead again, almost in a circular motion if seen from the side of the body. Since the next downbeat occurs on the first syllable of "many", the hand must move up on the word "as". Therefore, the cut-off for the 1-beat at the end of "Amen" should move to the right.

Example 180

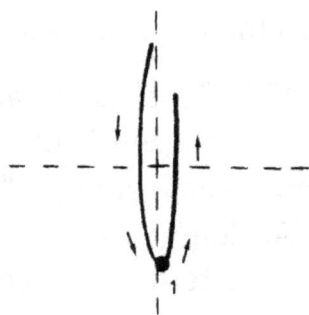

From the downbeat on "many" to the downbeat on "baptized", there are three half-note values. Thus, a 3-pattern will be used on "many". From the downbeat on "baptized" to the downbeat on "Christ", there are two-and-a-half half-note values. On "baptized", then, an **extended** 2-pattern will be used. Since a secondary accent is found on the first syllable of "into", this will be the point where the second half of the 2-pattern (where the hand will move up) will begin. The extension, then, is on the first half of the pattern. To get the feel of the extension, count "1, 2" on each half of the 2-pattern; that is, "1, 2" as your hand moves down and "1, 2" as your hand moves up. Then, without changing the speed of your counting, count "1, 2, 3" on the downbeat. To do this, you will have to **extend** your hand further down on the downbeat, at the point of the curve of the backwards "J". Practice doing this while singing, "baptized", giving the first syllable a half-note value and the second syllable a quarter-note value. Start bringing your hand up (for the second half of the beat" on the two syllables for "into".

From "Christ" to "put", there are two half-note values, as there are between "put" and the second word "Christ", and again between "Christ" and the third syllable of "Alleluia". All of these downbeats, then, will have 2-patterns. Since this hymn is repeated, and the music calls for an upbeat on "as" back at the beginning, a 4-pattern should be used on the third syllable of "Alleluia", except for the last time, when a 3-pattern will be used to end the hymn. This will result in the last syllable of "Alleluia", which is an unaccented syllable, being directed to the right, enabling a smooth cut-off.

The following example illustrates the hymn again, with markings for the downbeats and beat patterns to be used. The arrow with a dot above it in parentheses at the beginning stands for the drop preparation beat. The marking of "x2" over the word "baptized" indicates an extended 2-pattern. The little notch over the word "into" shows where the second half of the 2-pattern (where your hand comes back up) begins. On "Alleluia", the 4-pattern is to be used, except for the final time, where the 3-pattern is indicated.

Example 181

This one example contains all the elements needed to direct the chant style of conducting. It is important to reiterate that where the primary textual accents occur is where the downbeats will be placed. Then, calculating how many beats are between each downbeat will determine what type of beat pattern will be assigned at each downbeat. Determining the preparation beat is vital to a smooth entrance. The use of a drop preparation, a 1-beat, and an extended beat may be called for, at times. Finally, a smooth cut-off guards against an abrupt ending to the singing. There are many different styles of cut-offs. The following example illustrates one that is both smooth and does not call attention to itself. It is done by keeping the hand palm down, and slightly bouncing the bottom of the palm. The cadence syllable is the last one sung.

Example 182

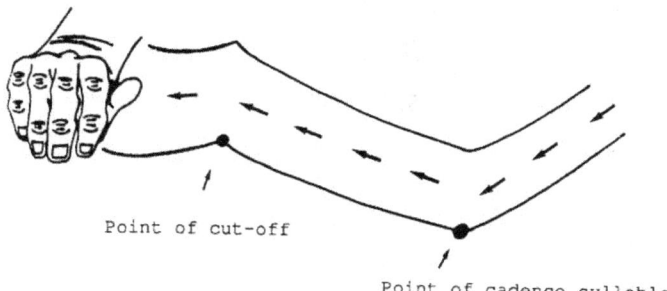

C. STIKHERA STYLE

The stikhera style of conducting is used when singing stikhera (verses) in which there are many syllables on one tone (recitative), followed by held tones at the cadence. The beginning of the verse would begin the same as a hymn in the chant style; that is, the first downbeat would be identified, and the four directions of the beat pattern would be backed up until reaching the preparation beat. For the recitative portion of the verse, a more subdued version of the 1-pattern would be called for. The conductor's hand would "bob" downward on the accented syllables, as a buoy bobs on water.

Example 183

Before assigning beat patterns to the cadences, it is necessary to identify where the held tones would occur according to the *musical* pattern of the tone being sung and the *textual* accents occurring at the beginning and end of the verses.

Example 184

Accept our evening prayers, O holy Lord.

Grant us remission of our sins, //

For You alone have manifested Your Resurrection to the world.

The double virgule at the end of the second line (**//**) indicates that this line is the last phrase pattern before the cadence phrase.

Using the musical patterns for Russian stikhera tone 1, this text can be marked as follows.

Example 185

Ac__cept__ our evening prayers, O __ho__ly Lord.

Grant us re__mis__sion of our sins, //

For You alone have manifested Your Resur__rec__tion to the world.

Analyzing this stikheron using the stikhera style, we find that the initial accent is on the second syllable of "accept". A drop preparation would be a good choice, since the first syllable would only use half a beat, using the half note as the basic beat, as is customary to do in the stikhera style. The secondary accent would be on the first syllable of "evening". An extended 1-beat on the second syllable of "accept" would be appropriate. Another secondary accent occurs on prayers. These can be marked by vertical notches (|). It would be at these points that the smaller 1-beat would "bob" down as you direct the choir. Another extended 1-beat could be assigned to the first syllable of "holy", ensuring a downbeat on "Lord".

On the second line, "grant" is a secondary, recitative accent, as is the word "of". Therefore, assigning an extended 2-beat to the second syllable of "remission" would bring the hand back up (for the second half of the beat) on the word "of". Since this line is not a complete sentence, but is completed by the third line, there should be no break in the singing or breathing at this point in the music. By assigning an extended 1-beat to "sins" at the end of the second line, the hand will come down for the secondary accent on "You" at the beginning of the third line. Other secondary accents in this line are the second syllable of "alone", the first and third syllables of "manifested", and the first syllable of "Resurrection". Using an extended 2-beat on the third syllable of "Resurrection" will bring about the desired downbeat on the word "world".

The following example illustrates how the choir director's sheet might be marked for directing this stikheron.

Example 186

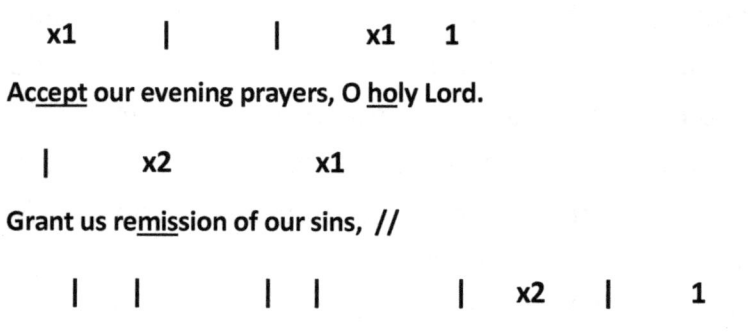

By using the subtle 1-beat for the secondary accents of the recitative and actual beat patterns for entrances and cadences, the music of the stikhera style is smoothly sung while properly accentuating the text.

D. REHEARSALS

The purpose of the choir rehearsal is to master the musical skills necessary for the celebration of the liturgical services, to the point where these skills become almost second nature, so that, during the services, concentration can be transferred from the music to the service itself (the words of the hymns, the liturgical prayers, litanies, and lectionary readings). In other words, the singers, in order to celebrate the service, need to enter into the service or, rather, allow the service to enter into them. This is not possible if one is concentrating on a melody that has not been adequately mastered, or giving pitches, or trying to figure out which beat patterns to use in directing a particular hymn. The rehearsal, then, means **preparation**.

Liturgical singing is a **ministry** of the Church. As such, and to keep this fact in perspective, it is appropriate to begin the rehearsal with the singing of an opening hymn, such as "O Heavenly King". This is done with everyone, including the choir director, facing the icon (or iconastasis, if rehearsing in the church building). Likewise, the rehearsal should close similarly, by singing a hymn such as the Hymn to the Theotokos.

An important item for a good rehearsal is the preparation of the choir director. The rehearsal itself being a preparation for singing the liturgical services, this involves a "preparation of the preparation" on the part of the director. **Total** familiarity with all parts of all hymns to be rehearsed is necessary if the rehearsal is to be the mastery of the music by the singers, and not the director. Selection of hymns to be rehearsed, with an idea of what needs special attention and how much rehearsal time will be spent on each hymn, should be planned out ahead of time. A constructive choir rehearsal should not last more than an hour and a half. More time than that will lead to fatigue on the part of the singers and, subsequently, a lack of attention and effectiveness in accomplishing more. Upcoming feasts and liturgical seasons (Great Lent, the Pentecostarion, Christmas Lent, etc.) will determine much of the material that will be covered. Many choir directors save the bulk of introducing new material for the summer season after Pentecost, when special material for feast days is not as prevalent as the rest of the year.

One effective method for the rehearsal is to go over the more simple material to be sung, while the singers are still "warming up". Once their voices and attention have been prepared, the rehearsing of more difficult arrangements will be more constructive.

Before singing and rehearsing the music itself, it is very beneficial to go over the **text** of the hymn being sung. This helps focus the attention on the **reality** of the words, the "content" of the text that the words are expressing. This aids tremendously in helping the singers to prayfully celebrate the services from the heart. In addition to this, review of the text without the music also calls attention to the **rhythm** of the text, that is, where the accents naturally occur in the text. This makes it easier to articulate and emphasize the text properly during the singing. The way it is said should be the way it is sung.

Going over the melody first in a new arrangement focuses everyone's attention on which voice contains the melody part. This helps the singers of the other parts to keep the function of their part (melody harmonization, roots of chords, etc.) in perspective, so as not to overpower the melody. Having all singers, at times, sing the melody (and other parts, when they are being rehearsed) keeps everyone actively involved in the rehearsal and reduces disciplinary problems.

Difficult passages in the music can be efficiently mastered by a process known as "woodshedding". **Woodshedding** involves "whittling" the problem area in the music down to the particular notes that are troublesome. It may be only a difficult interval or leap between two notes in a part. Isolating the music down to only the problem notes allows greater concentration on the area in question, and also aids in a quicker mastery over the difficult part. Repeating the **corrected** notes a few times reinforces singing the passage the right way. Once the isolated section has been mastered, the music surrounding the troublesome notes (the few notes and words just before and after the problem area) should then be included. This, also, should be repeated a few times for reinforcement. After this, adding the rest of the four parts in singing the problem area will help in seeing and hearing how the difficult notes fit in the context of the rest of the hymn.

EXERCISES • CHAPTER 8

Mastery of the beat patterns used in conducting should be the initial task of the director. After this, review, practice, and application of the chant and stikhera styles of conducting should be repeated. The more you practice, the easier this becomes, and the more confident you will become in directing your choir for having mastered these skills. Taking a vocal conducting course, or having a more experienced choir director guide you along, can also prove to be beneficial.

9
THEOLOGY OF ORTHODOX LITURGICAL MUSIC

Theology is defined as words adequate to God. It is the experience of our Faith, lived out in liturgy and in our daily lives. Theology, then, is not an academic enterprise promulgated by stuffy intellectuals in university libraries. It is the articulation of that which makes up our very being and of everything in creation. It is "the expression of our **experience** of being baptized into the life of the Father and the Son and the Holy Spirit".[1] To use St Paul's term, it is our life "***in Christ***".

A theology of our liturgical music, then, is the expression and explanation of it as it really is, as it really functions, and as it is really experienced in its proper perspective.

---

[1] Archimandrite Vasileios, *Hymn of Entry*, SVS (St Vladimir's Seminary) Press, Crestwood, NY, 1984, p. 19.

A. THE HOLY TRINITY

Everything in creation is an expression, a revelation, of God. To understand something in creation, liturgical music, for example, we must first understand God as He really is. This is revealed in the dogma of the Holy Trinity. The word **dogma** means official teaching,[2] and is something that is revealed by God to the Church, usually over a long period of time. The dogma of the Holy Trinity took four hundred years to formulate.

According to Orthodox doctrine, the one God of the Christian Faith is the Person of God the Father.[3] It is **not** the Trinity. This is not to say that the Son and the Holy Spirit are not divine. They are equally divine with the same divinity as that of the Father, and are as eternal and perfect as the Father is. They share the same **nature** as the Father, but They are different **Persons**. They are **what** the Father is, but not **Who** He

---

[2]Hopko, Thomas, *The Orthodox Faith: Volume I: Doctrine (An Elementary Handbook on the Orthodox Church)*, Department of Religious Education, Orthodox Church in America, New York, NY, 1971 (hereafter referred to as "*Doctrine*"), p. 12.
[3]Ibid, p. 139.

is. "Hear, O Israel, the Lord, He is God, the Lord, He is **One**" (Dt 6:4).

Being the one God, the Father is the **Source** of all that there is, **including** the Son and the Holy Spirit. This is why They are referred to as "the Son *of* God" and "the Spirit *of* God". Being the Source and Father is the main characteristic of God the Father. He is the **Content** of everything.

The Son of God, the Word (**Logos** in Greek), is the very **Expression** of the Father's Own Being. He is the Image of the invisible God (Col 1:15), the very Icon of His being. The Son Himself reveals that to us: "He who has seen Me has seen the Father" (Jn 14:9). The Son expresses the very Content of God.

The Holy Spirit, the Spirit of God, is the Communicator of the Life of the Father, the **Giver** of this Life.[4] He is the Activator, the **Vivifier**, Who communicates, activates, and electrifies the Life of God, making it be **alive**. The Holy Spirit vivifies the Life, the Content of God the Father.

The Holy Spirit, along with vivifying the Life of God, has other Personal characteristics. He is, in one sense, the "hidden Person" of the Holy Trinity: "He

---

[4]Stikheron to the Holy Spirit, "O Heavenly King". See also Hopko, Thomas, *The Spirit of God*, Morehouse-Barlow Company, Inc, Wilton, CT, 1976.

remains **unrevealed, hidden**, so to speak, by the gift in order that this gift which He imparts may be fully ours, adapted to our persons".[5] The Son is revealed to us directly as the Man, Jesus Christ. The Father is revealed to us in the Person of the Son, Who is the perfect Image of the Father. The Person of the Holy Spirit is revealed to us more subtlely, in the multiplicity of persons who make up the Church: "...for the multitude of saints will be His image".[6]

Another Personal characteristic of the Holy Spirit, however, is that of *inspiration*. Even though He remains humbly "hidden", it is through His inspiration that the prophets spoke the Word of God revealed to them, that the human authors of the Books of the Bible communicated the Word of God to us *in words*. It is through His inspiration that Christ was baptized, that He was led into the wilderness to be tempted, that He cast out devils, healed the sick, fed the multitude in the wilderness, raised the dead, and was led to the Cross.

---

[5]Lossky, Vladimir, *The Mystical Theology of the Eastern Church*, SVS Press, Crestwood, NY, 1976, pp. 166-167.
[6]Ibid, p. 173.

B. THE TRINITARIAN DIMENSION OF ORTHODOX LITURGICAL MUSIC

If everything in creation is an expression of God, then each thing has a trinitarian dimension to it. This is true, also, of liturgical music. There are, therefore, three aspects of liturgical music. The first of these is the **content** of the hymn, the reality that is being expressed in word and song. This is analogous to the Person of God the Father, Who is the Content of everything. This is also true because the content of every hymn, whether it be a doxology praising God or a troparion of the life of one of His saints, is **God Himself**.

The second characteristic of liturgical music is the **word**. Without words, the music carries no meaning in and of itself (this is why instruments are canonically forbidden in the Orthodox Church; every sound must have a meaning, and meaning can only verbally be communicated in words). This is analogous to the Person of the Son, Who is the Word of God, Who reveals God to us. As the Word of God leads us to the Content of divinity, to the Person of God the Father ("No one comes to the Father but by Me" [Jn 14:6]), so the words of the hymn lead us to its content, to communion with God.

The third characteristic of liturgical music is the *music* itself. This is analogous to the Person of the Holy Spirit, Who vivifies and gives Life to all, even God. The music gives life and vivifies the words of the hymn, leading us through them to the content, to God. We approach and commune with God the Father through the Son in the Holy Spirit. We approach and commune with the content of our hymnography through the words in the music.

C. MUSIC AND TEXT

This analogy can be contemplated more deeply. If the words of our hymnography are analogous to the Personal characteristics of the Son and the music is analogous to the Personal characteristics of the Holy Spirit, what do the Son's and the Holy Spirit's characteristics say about the characteristics of the words and the music.

The Son of God is undoubtedly the Person of the Holy Trinity Who reveals Himself the most directly. It is the Son Who was incarnate of the Virgin; it is the Son Who was baptized, walked among men, taught, healed, exorcized, raised the dead, was crucified, buried, resurrected, ascended into Heaven, and sent the Comforter into the world. Since He is the image of the invisible God (Col 1:15), then God Himself (the Father) is invisible, as is the Holy Spirit. "No man has seen God at any time; the only Son, Who is in the loins of the Father, He has made Him known" (Jn 1:18).

If, then, the Son is the One Who is in the forefront, Who stands out and is primary (no one comes to the Father but by Him, and it is He (the Son) Who sends the Spirit), **then it is the words, the text, of our hymnography that must be in the forefront, that must stand out and be primary!**

Likewise, the Holy Spirit is the Person of the Trinity Who is "hidden", Who is in the background. Yet, while not calling attention to Himself, He nevertheless is the One Who vivifies, makes alive, and inspires. Therefore, the musical element of our hymnography must *not* call attention to itself, must not overpower and cloud the text and the meaning of the text. It is not the music that leads us to the content of the hymnography (the Gospels states that "No one comes to the Father but by Me [the Son]"; it does not say that "No one comes to the Father but by the Spirit"), but rather, the music makes the text come alive and, through that vivification, inspires us to enter into the text, embracing, contemplating, and praying with the text, to make our hearts one with its content.

The difficult task of the choir director (after mastering the musically technical skills outlined in this book), the **cross** that needs to be taken up at each service and rehearsal, is to walk the narrow road of allowing the music to vivify the text, to inspire us to enter into its reality, without overpowering, clouding, or dominating the forefront of our hymnography. This is realized in many ways. First of all, it is realized in the choice of arrangements to be sung. Many arrangements are **not** liturgical for the very reason that the music is so ornate that the text and its content, the prayer, the doxology, the enumeration of the Faith, is lost or buried. Other arrangements may be musically appropriate, but the way the music is set to the text takes away from its contemplation by misaccenting the words. Putting half notes on unaccented syllables makes the singing cumbersome, unprayerful, and non-liturgical.

Once appropriate, liturgical arrangements have been chosen, the choir director must be watchful that the execution of the singing is not done in a manner that is sentimental, what modern jargon would call "schmaltzy". Using extreme emotionalism in the style of singing distracts and detracts from the concentration of the words and their content. There is a unity, a harmony among the three Persons of the Holy Trinity. There also needs to be a unity, a balance, a harmony between the three aspects (content, text, and music) of our Orthodox hymnography.

D. LITURGICAL MUSIC AND ESCHATOLOGY

Finally, our Orthodox liturgical music is just that, it is **liturgical**. **Liturgy** means "common work" or "common action",[7] and our hymnography is an essential part of that work. It is only when the people of God gather together, assemble **as Church** do they **constitute** the Church, becoming the very Body of Christ which is the Church. And it is only in these divine gatherings, within this divine Assembly that our hymnography manifests and becomes what it is in its very nature, **liturgical** music.

What, then, is goal, the main thrust, of liturgy and, therefore, of liturgical music? What takes place at the Divine Liturgy? What is the apex of this service that is called "the Eucharist"? Is it not the Eucharist itself, the partaking of the Body and Blood of Christ,

---

[7]Hopko, Thomas, *The Orthodox Faith: Volume II: Worship (An Elementary Handbook on the Orthodox Church)*, Department of Religious Education, Orthodox Church in America, New York, NY, 1972, p. 154.

what has been called the Sacrament of sacraments? And, if this is so, why has this sacrament been given to us? Why did Christ "institute" the Holy Supper before His life-saving Passion? The answer is given to us by the Lord Himself during that very Meal: "And I assign to You, as My Father assigned to Me, a **Kingdom**, that you may eat and drink at **My** Table in **My** Kingdom" (Lk 22:29-30). It is this Kingdom that is the Goal, the End, and the Fulfillment of all things. It is this **Eschaton** (the Last Things) that is the focus and whose content is the Kingdom of God, the Life lived **in Christ**, in perfect communion with God the Father and the Holy Spirit. Thus, this Kingdom, which is given to us in the Church, the Church Herself, Her life, Her liturgy, and Her music, are all **eschatological**. It is this Life in communion with God in His Kingdom that is the **content** of our Orthodox hymnography.

"And, when they had sung a hymn, they went to the Mount of Olives" (Mt 26:30; Mk 14:26). From the beginning, music has been inexorably linked with the Eucharist and with the Kingdom. **Eucharist** means "thanksgiving", and **thanksgiving** is at the very heart of this Life of the Kingdom. In thanksgiving, Christ fed the multitudes in the wilderness, offered up prayer to His Father, and accepted voluntarily His life-saving Passion. It is in and through this **ministry** of liturgical music that we enter into this thanksgiving of Christ, making it our own and the very content of our life: "...but be filled with the Spirit, addressing one another in psalms and hymns and spiritual songs, singing and making melody to the Lord with all your heart, always and for everything giving thanks in the Name of our Lord Jesus Christ to God the Father" (Eph 5:19-20).[8]

---

[8]Epistle reading for the second Day of the Holy Trinity, the Day of the Holy Spirit.

ANSWERS TO EXERCISES

1. MUSIC READING

1.

2.

3.

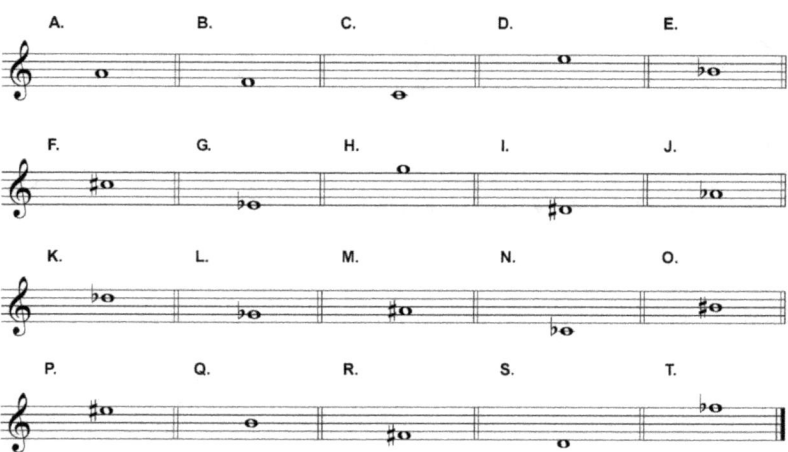

Answers to Exercises

4.

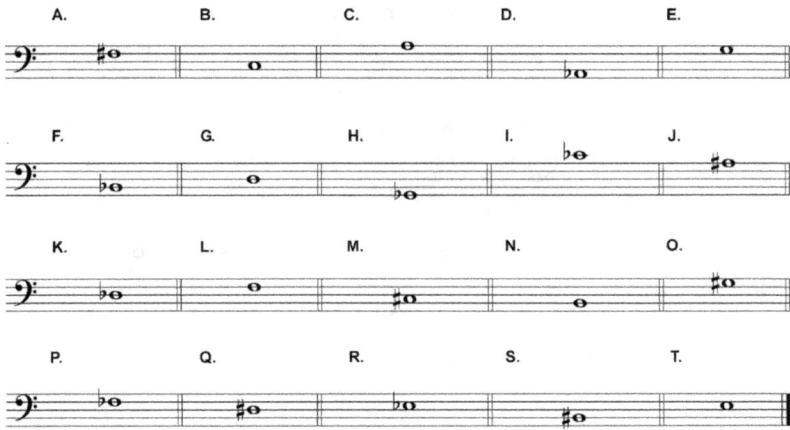

5.

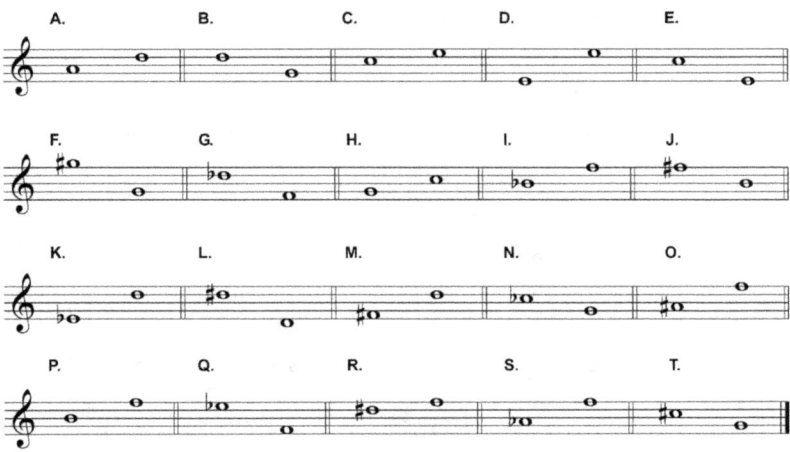

6.

7.

8.

A)	*E*	B)	*A*	C)	*G*	D)	*B*
E)	*G*	F)	*D#*	G)	*Ab*	H)	*D*
I)	*Fb*	J)	*C#*	K)	*Bb*	L)	*A#*
M)	*C#*	N)	*Gb*	O)	*E#*	P)	*F*
Q)	*Bb*	R)	*F#*	S)	*Eb*	T)	*G#*

9.

A)	4th	B)	8th [octave]			C)	5th
D)	4th	E)	5th	F)	7th	G)	5th
H)	2nd	I)	5th	J)	3rd	K)	5th
L)	5th	M)	7th	N)	4th	O)	7th
P)	3rd	Q)	4th	R)	3rd	S)	4th
T)	8th						

230   *Elementary Music Theory for Orthodox Liturgical Singing*

10.

A) 2ⁿᵈ	B) 8ᵗʰ [octave]				C) 4ᵗʰ	
D) 3ʳᵈ	E) 3ʳᵈ	F) 2ⁿᵈ		G) 4ᵗʰ		
H) 7ᵗʰ	I) 4ᵗʰ	J) 6ᵗʰ		K) 4ᵗʰ		
L) 4ᵗʰ	M) 2ⁿᵈ	N) 5ᵗʰ		O) 2ⁿᵈ		
P) 4ᵗʰ	Q) 5ᵗʰ	R) 6ᵗʰ		S) 5ᵗʰ		
T) 8ᵗʰ						

11.

12.

13.

A) quarter note   B) half note   C) eighth note
D) whole note   E) whole rest   F) quarter rest
G) eighth rest   H) half rest
I) two eighth notes, separated
J) two eighth notes, connected
K)   eighth rest, quarter rest, eighth rest, half rest
L)   half note, quarter rest, eighth note, eighth rest
M)   eighth note, quarter rest, half note, eighth rest
N)   quarter rest, half rest, quarter rest
O)   quarter note, half note, quarter note

P) eighth rest, quarter note, eighth rest, quarter note, quarter rest
Q) half rest, eighth note, quarter rest, eighth rest
R) quarter rest, half note, eighth rest, quarter note
S) quarter rest, eighth note, quarter note, eighth rest, quarter rest
T) quarter note, eighth rest, eighth note, half rest

14.

A) four beats per minute, quarter note gets one beat
B) two beats per minute, half note gets one beat
C) three beats per minute, quarter note gets one beat
D) nine beats per minute, half note gets one beat
E) seven beats per minute, eighth note gets one beat
F) eleven beats per minute, quarter note gets one beat
G) thirteen beats per minute, half note gets one beat
H) two beats per minute, half note gets one beat

Answers to Exercises

I) seven beats per minute, half note gets one beat
J) three beats per minute, eighth note gets one beat
K) twelve beats per minute, quarter note gets one beat
L) nine beats per minute, eighth note gets one beat
M) four beats per minute, half note gets one beat
N) eight beats per minute, half note gets one beat
O) thirteen beats per minute, quarter note gets one beat
P) eleven beats per minute, eighth note gets one beat
Q) five beats per minute, quarter note gets one beat
R) three beats per minute, half note gets one beat
S) five beats per minute, half note gets one beat
T) four beats per minute, quarter note gets one beat

15.

A) music – sound and silence organized in time.
B) beat – a rhythmic pulse.
C) meter – grouping of beats.
D) quarter note – a note with a black (filled-in) note head and a stem, which takes up a quarter of a measure in $\frac{4}{4}$ time.
E) basic beat – total time span from the beginning of one beat until the beginning of the next beat.
F) measure – a grouping of the rhythmic patterns into a cycle of a specific number of beats.
G) bar line – the vertical line which separates one measure from another.
H) time signature – the set of numbers at the beginning of the line of music: the top number tells us how many beats are in a measure and the bottom number tells us what kind of note gets one beat.
I) common time – the meter of $\frac{4}{4}$ time, which is one of the most common meters in Western music.

Answers to Exercises

J) quarter rest – a rest that looks like a z-shaped zigzag, that takes up a quarter of a measure in $\frac{4}{4}$ time.

K) cut time – the meter of $\frac{2}{2}$ time, which can be said to "cut" the meter of $\frac{4}{4}$ time in half; also called "alla breve".

L) pitch – the highness or lowness of a sound resulting from vibrations per second.

M) frequency – speed of vibrations per second of a sound.

N) octave – space between two notes of the same letter name.

O) flat – a b-shaped symbol that, coming before a note, lowers it one half-step in pitch.

P) sharp – a number sign-shaped symbol that, coming before a note, raises it one half-step in pitch.

Q) staff – the set of five lines and four spaces between these lines on which music is shown.

R) treble clef – the **G**-shaped symbol at the beginning of a line of music that encompasses the pitches in the treble range of voices: sopranos, altos, and (sometimes) tenors; also called the **G**-clef.

236 *Elementary Music Theory for Orthodox Liturgical Singing*

S) bass clef – the backwards-**C**-shaped symbol at the beginning of a line of music that encompasses the pitches in the bass range of voices: tenors and basses; also called the **F**-clef.

T) interval – the distance between two tones.

2. KEYS AND SCALES

1.

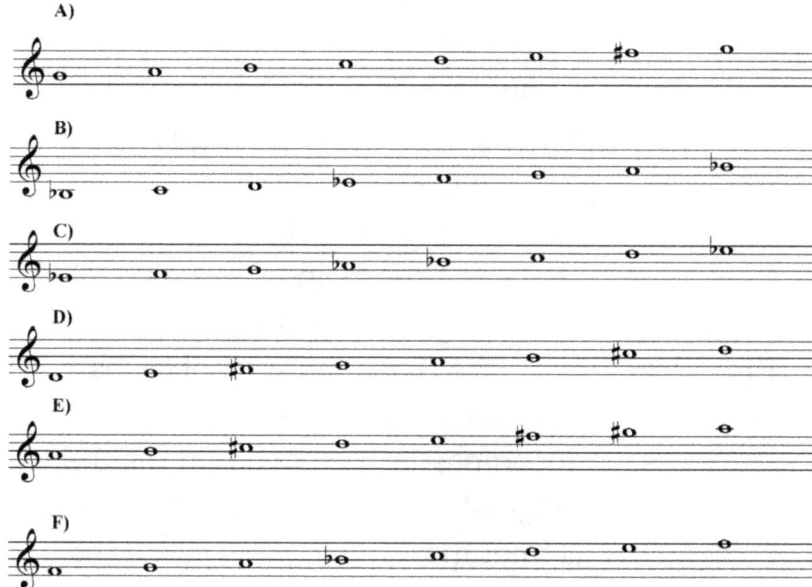

Answers to Exercises

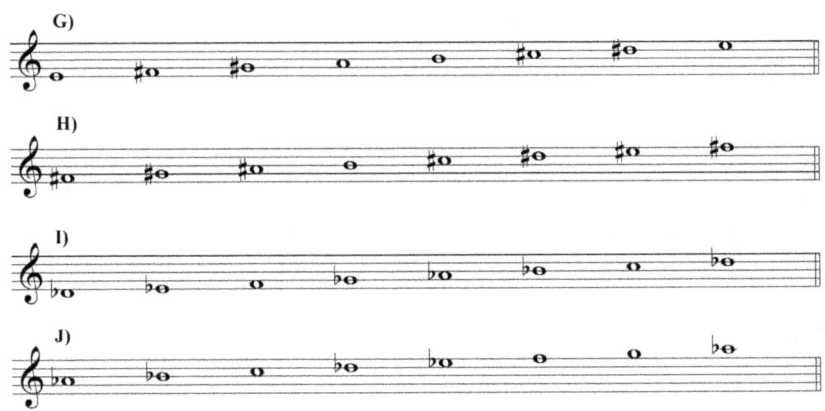

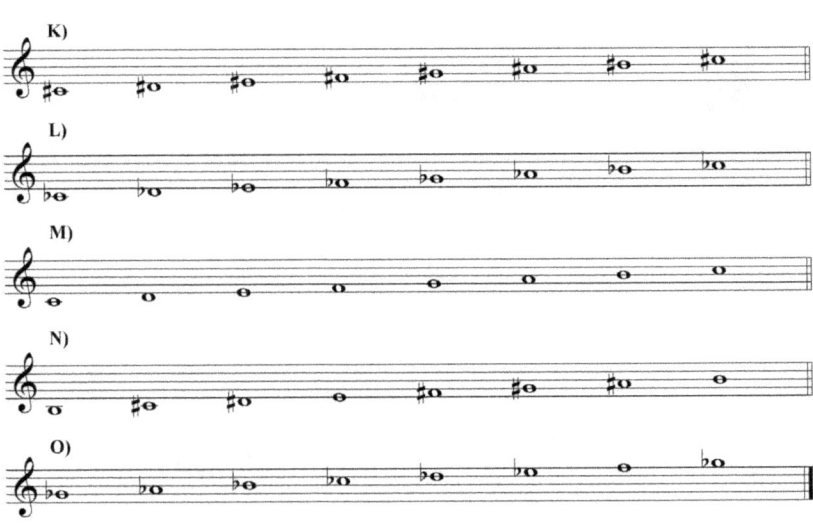

2.

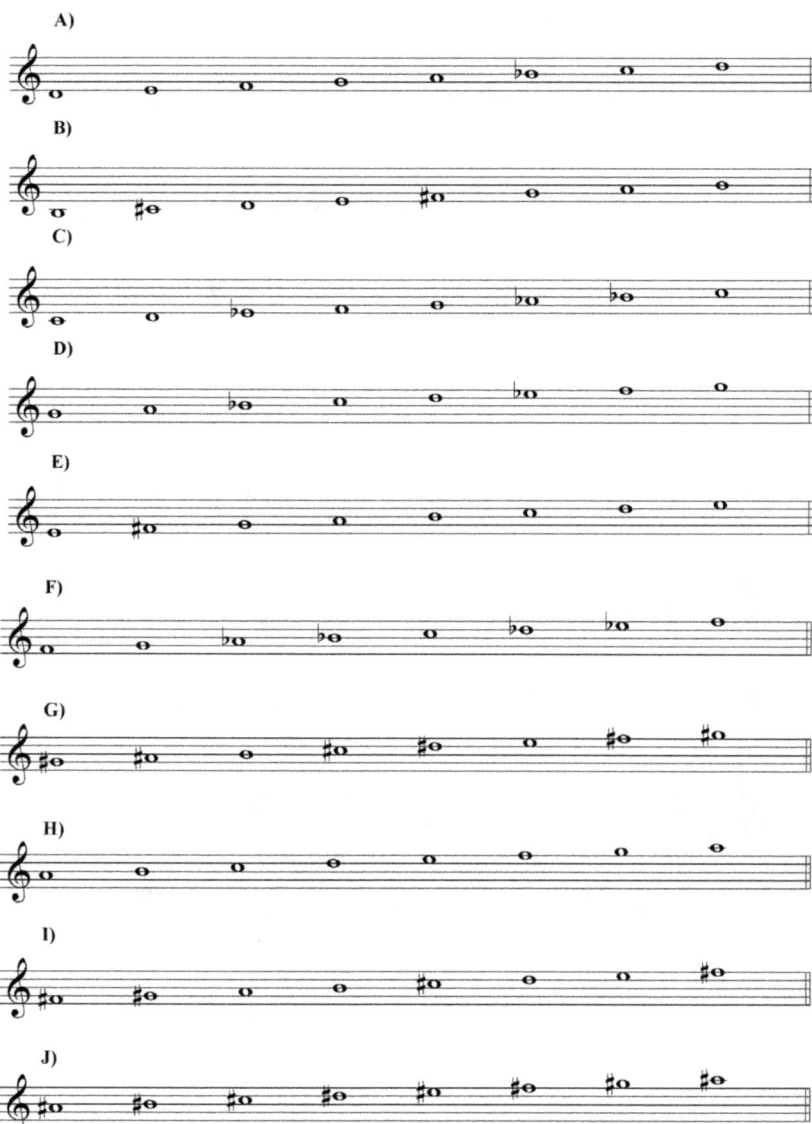

Answers to Exercises   239

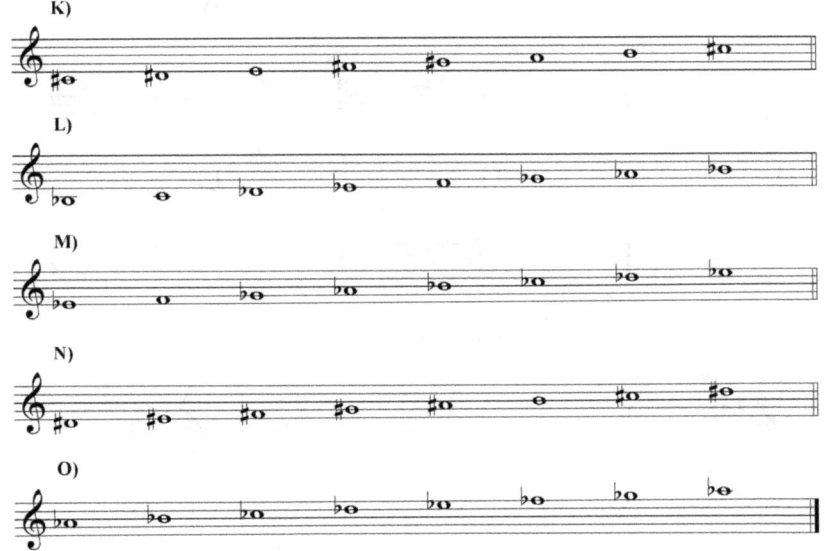

3. **W**hole, **W**hole, **H**alf, **W**hole, **W**hole, **W**hole, **H**alf.

4. **W**hole, **H**alf, **W**hole, **W**hole, **H**alf, **W**hole, **W**hole.

5.

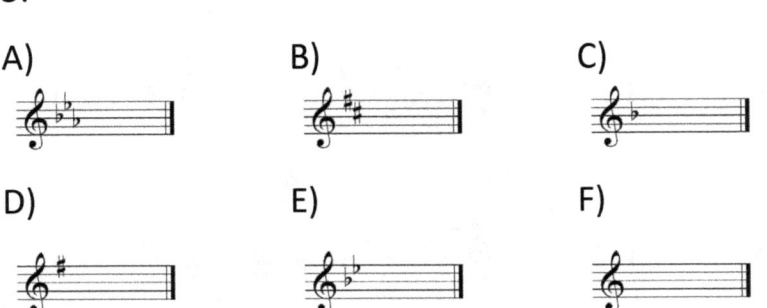

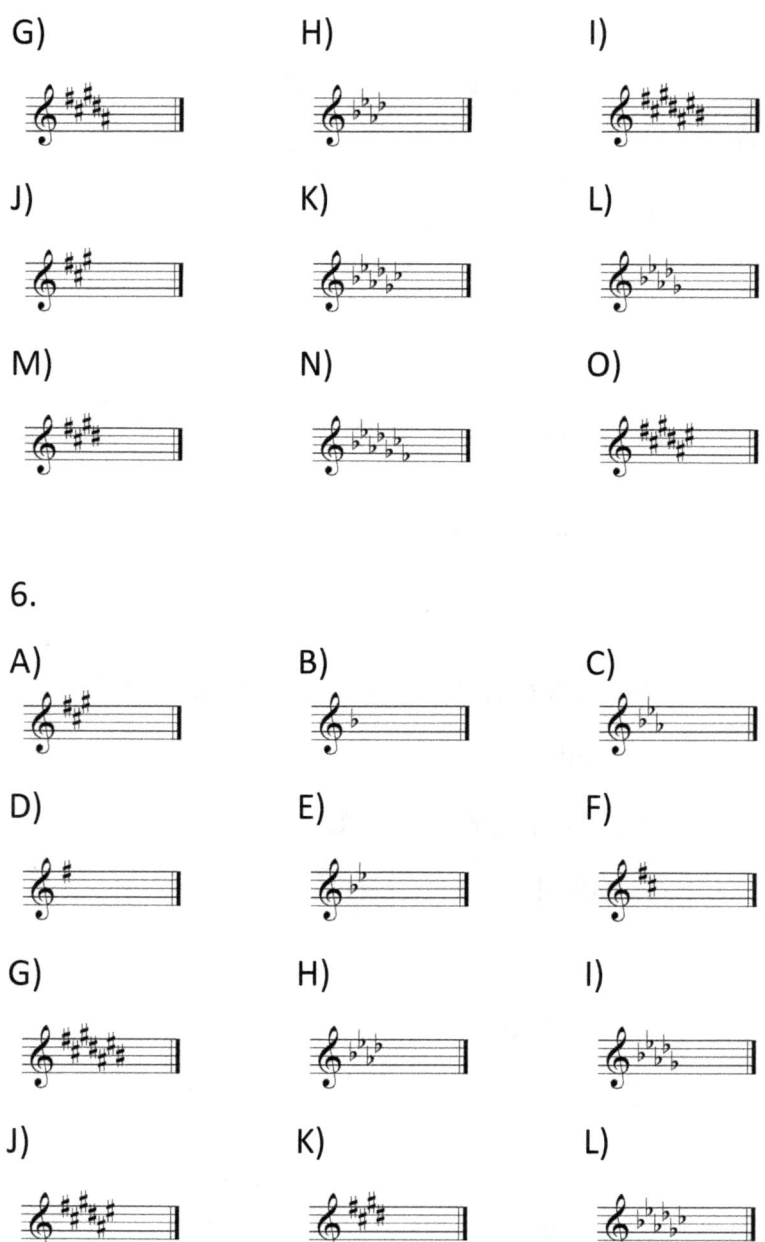

Answers to Exercises

M) [staff with 6 sharps]   N) [empty staff]   O) [staff with 4 flats]

7.

A)	E^b	B)	D	C)	A
D)	$G^\#$	E)	G	F)	D
G)	E	H)	E^b	I)	B
J)	$D^\#$	K)	E^b	L)	$C^\#$
M)	$F^\#$	N)	B^b	O)	G
P)	F	Q)	$C^\#$	R)	A
S)	G	T)	E		

8.

A)	d	B)	a	C)	e
D)	e^b	E)	g	F)	d
G)	a^b	H)	f^b	I)	b
J)	$g^\#$	K)	e	L)	a
M)	d^b	N)	a	O)	$c^\#$
P)	$f^\#$	Q)	e^b	R)	$f^\#$
S)	g	T)	g^b		

9.

A)	**Do**	B)	**Mi**	C)	**Sol**
D)	**Ti**	E)	**Fa**	F)	**Re**
G)	**La**				

10.

A)	**La**	B)	**Fa**	C)	**Do**
D)	**Mi**	E)	**Sol**	F)	**Re**
G)	**Ti**				

3. TRIADS

1.

Answers to Exercises

2.

A) major 3rd, minor 3rd, perfect 5th.
B) minor 3rd, major 3rd, perfect 5th.
C) minor 3rd, minor 3rd, diminished 5th.
D) major 3rd, major 3rd, augmented 5th.
E) minor 3rd, major 3rd, minor 3rd, perfect 5th, minor 7th.

3.

If a triad consists, from the bottom up, of a major 3rd, a minor 3rd, and a perfect 5th, it is a major triad. Also, if all the notes of the triad exist naturally in the major key of the root of the chord, it is a major triad.

4.

If a triad consists, from the bottom up, of a minor 3rd, a major 3rd, and a perfect 5th, it is a minor triad. Also, if all the notes of the triad exist naturally in the minor key of the root of the chord, it is a minor triad.

5.

With the following musical answers, the notes of the triad for the upper three voices are interchangeable. What is most important, and cannot be changed, is the note in the bass voice.

Answers to Exercises

6.

With the following musical answers, the notes of the triad for the upper three voices are interchangeable. What is most important, and cannot be changed, is the note in the bass voice.

7.

With the following musical answers, the notes of the 7th chord for the upper three voices are interchangeable. What is most important, and cannot be changed, is the note in the bass voice.

8.

Take the tonic note of the major key, that falls on **Do**, and go to the note that falls on **La**, and you have the relative minor key. Or, take the note that falls on **Do** and go back two notes, and you have the relative minor key. For example, in **F** major, **F** falls on **Do**. Go either to the note that falls on **La** or go back two notes from **F**. In both cases, you come to **D**. Therefore, the relative minor key from **F** major is **d** minor.

9.

I   ii   iii   IV   V   vi   vii°   I.

10.

I   ii°   III   iv   V   VI   VII   i.

BIBLIOGRAPHY

Music

Christ, William; DeLone, Richard; Kliewer, Vernon; Rowell, Lewis; and Thomson, William; **Materials and Structure of Music, Volume 1**, 2nd Edition, Prentice Hall, Englewood Cliffs, New Jersey, 1972. Introductory material presented on a college freshman language level.

Jones, George Thaddeus, **Music Theory**, Barnes and Noble (Harper and Row), New York, New York, 1974. Easier reading than **Materials**, but not as complete.

Lamb, Gordon H., **Choral Techniques**, William C. Brown Company, Dubuque, Iowa, 1976. Written for teaching singing in schools, it is nevertheless helpful, especially in the area of rehearsal technique.

Rudolf, Max, The **Grammar of Conducting**, 2nd Edition, Schirmer Books, Macmillan Publishing Company, Inc., New York, New York, 1980. The most complete conducting book written, both for choral and instrumental music.

Liturgical Music

von Gardner, Johann, ***Russian Church Singing, Volume 1: Orthodox Worship and Hymnography***, St Vladimir's Seminary (SVS) Press, Crestwood, New York, 1980. A must for all liturgical musicians, it presents the structure and rubrics of the services of the Orthodox Church, as well as examining the essence of liturgical music.

Wellecz, Egon, ***A History of Byzantine Music and Hymnography***, 2nd Edition, Oxford at the Clarendon Press, Oxford, England, 1980. The authoritative work on Byzantine chant.

Douglas, Winfred, ***Church Music in History and Practice***, Charles Scribner's Sons, New York, New York, 1937. Written by a Protestant, it is a valuable book on liturgical singing, particularly in the relationship of music and text.

Theology

Hopko, Father Thomas, ***The Orthodox Faith: An Elementary Handbook on the Orthodox Church***, Department of Religious Education, Orthodox Church in America, New York, New York, 1971. Written in four volumes (***I: Doctrine***; ***II: Worship***; ***III: Bible and Church History***; ***IV: Spirituality***), this series presents the teachings of the Orthodox Faith in a clear, easy-to-read format that is very understandable. Illustrated.

Schmemann, Father Alexander, ***Introduction to Liturgical Theology***, SVS Press, Crestwood, New York, 1986. A deep book that should be re-read many times, it is, however, invaluable for a correct perspective of the liturgical situation in the Orthodox Church.

Ware, Archimandrite Kallistos (Timothy), ***The Orthodox Church***, Penguin Books, New York, New York, 1963. A thorough handbook of the Orthodox Church, it discusses its history, faith, and worship.

Music Books

Drillock, David; Erickson, John H.; and Erickson, Helen Breslich, eds.; *The Divine Liturgy*, SVS Press, Crestwood, New York, 1982. Contains settings of hymns for the Liturgy from various traditions. Also by SVS Press are: *Holy Week: Volumes 1, 2, and 3*; *Pascha: The Resurrection of Christ*; and *The Liturgy of the Presanctified Gifts*.

Liturgical Books

Hapgood, Isabel Florence, *Service Book of the Holy Orthodox-Catholic Apostolic Church*, 4th Edition, Syrian Antiochian Orthodox Archdiocese, Brooklyn, New York, 1965. Although the translations are quite archaic, the book does present all the services of the Church.

Nassar, the late Reverend Seraphim, *Divine Prayers and Services of the Catholic Orthodox Church of Christ*, Antiochian Orthodox Christian Archdiocese, Englewood, New Jersey, 1979. Also archaic in textual usage, it nevertheless presents the rubrical propers of the liturgical services.

Ware, Archimandrite Kallistos and Mother Mary; ***The Festal Menaion***, Faber and Faber, London, England, 1969. Texts of the Twelve Major Feasts.

_____; ***The Lenten Triodion***, Faber and Faber, London, England, 1978. Texts of Great Lent, from the Sunday of the Publican and the Pharisee to Holy Saturday.

GLOSSARY OF TERMS

alla breve - also called ***cut time***, it refers to a time signature consisting of two beats per measure, with a half note getting one beat.

anacrusis - also called a ***pick-up note***, it is the beginning beat of a musical composition that does not begin on the first beat of the first full measure.

antecedent-consequent phrases - phrases which call for an answer; the antecedent phrase is the "question phrase", and the consequent phrase is the "answer phrase".

antiphonal singing - literally meaning "against the sound", it usually designates the use of two choirs in alternation.

augmented interval - a major or perfect interval that has been augmented (enlarged) one half step.

augmented triad - a triad consisting of two major 3rds and an augmented 5th.

bar line - the vertical line that separates one measure from another.

basic beat (duration) - the total time span from the beginning of one beat until the beginning of the next beat.

bass clef - also called the **F-clef**, it is the symbol at the beginning of the bass staff.

bass staff - the lower staff of the grand staff, which covers the bass range of voices, those of tenors and basses.

beat - a rhythmic pulse.

cadence - a musical ending or closing section.

cantor (canonarch) - a lead singer or reader.

chant - song; repetitive liturgical melody in which as many syllables are assigned to each tone as required.

chant style - a conducting style utilizing a combination of different meters, organized according to the text.

chord - a group of three or more alternate pitches, sounding simultaneously.

chord tones - notes belonging as members of a chord.

clef - the symbol at the beginning of a staff that identifies that staff.

common time - a time signature consisting of four beats per measure, with a quarter note getting one beat.

conducting plane - the area in which the conductor moves his or her arms.

contour - the shape of a phrase.

cut time - also called ***alla breve***, it refers to a time signature consisting of two beats per measure, with a half note getting one beat.

diminished interval - a minor or perfect interval that has been diminished (reduced) one half step.

diminished triad - a triad consisting of two minor 3rds and a diminished 5th.

dogma - an official teaching of the Church.

dominant - the tone a 5th above (or a 4th below) the tonic.

dotted note - a note with a dot following it, whereby the value of the note is increased by one-half.

downbeat - the first half of a beat, when the foot tapping the rhythm is going down to the floor.

drop preparation - a preparation beat used when beginning a hymn on the last half of a beat.

dynamics - the variation and contrast in the force and intensity (volume) of music.

eighth note - a type of note composed of a blackened (filled-in) note head, a stem, and a flag, which, in common time, takes up one-eighth of a measure in $\frac{4}{4}$ time.

Glossary of Terms

eighth rest - a rest shaped like the number 7 and, in common time, takes up one-eighth of a measure in $\frac{4}{4}$ time.

enharmonic - refers to two notes which are the same in pitch but have different letter names.

Eschaton - the Last Things; the Fulfillment of all in the Kingdom of God, which is ***eschatological***.

F-clef - also called the ***bass clef***, it is the symbol at the beginning of the bass staff.

The Father - He Who is God, Who is the Source of everything, both within the Holy Trinity (the Son and the Holy Spirit) and in creation; the First Person of the Holy Trinity.

first inversion - a chord with the 3rd in the bass.

Fixed Do system - the solfege system used primarily in Europe, where ***C*** is fixed as always being ***Do***, no matter what key the music is in.

flat - a musical symbol that lowers the pitch of a note by one half step.

4-pattern - a conducting pattern in which 4 beats are conducted in the following directional pattern: down, left, right, up.

free meter - the meter of the chant style of conducting, in which the music is not confined to the regularity of one strict meter.

G-clef - also called the **treble clef**, it is the symbol at the beginning of the treble staff.

God - the one God of the Christian Faith, the God of Abraham, Isaac, and Jacob, the Father Almighty, Who, by His very Nature, has a Son and a Holy Spirit.

grand (great) staff - the combination of the treble staff and the bass staff into one staff.

half note - a type of note composed of an open (not filled-in) note head and a stem, which, in common time, takes up one-half of a measure in $\frac{4}{4}$ time.

half rest - a rest which looks like a right-side-up hat, and which, in common time, takes up one-half of a measure in $\frac{4}{4}$ time.

half step - the smallest interval used in most Western music.

harmony - the chordal or vertical structure of a musical composition.

The Holy Spirit - the Spirit of God, Whose Personal characteristic it is to give Life to everything, even to God Himself; He is equally divine with the same Nature as the Father and the Son; the Third Person of the Holy Trinity.

homophony - music consisting of a single melodic line with harmonic accompaniment.

hymn - in general, any piece of liturgical song; specifically, a liturgical song whose poetic text offers praise or prayer to God.

interval - the distance between two tones.

intonation formulae - a pattern of notes or tones which function, most often, as a preparation or announcement of the mode of the melody of a Byzantine tone; if it comes between verses, it serves to link the recitation of the preceding verse with the verse that follows.

inversion - redistribution of chord tones out of root position.

ison - a repeated pitch that functions as a reference tone in Byzantine chant, to which the melody refers.

kanon tones - tones set to the texts of kanons, which occur primarily in Matins.

key - the tonal center of a Western musical composition.

key signature - the set of sharps or flats at the beginning of a musical composition.

leading tone - the tone a half step below the tonic, which leads up to it.

ledger line - a line above or below a staff on which to write notes.

liturgical - something which is, by its very nature, an element of the services of the Church.

liturgy - "common work" or "common action"; the central, eucharistic service of the Orthodox Church.

lower interval - an interval that moves down from a given note.

major interval - interval of a 2nd, 3rd, 6th, or 7th that occurs naturally in the major key of the root of the chord.

major scale - a scale whose pattern of whole steps and half steps is: **W**hole, **W**hole, **H**alf, **W**hole, **W**hole, **W**hole, **H**alf.

major triad - a triad consisting of a major 3rd, a minor 3rd, and a perfect 5th.

measure - a grouping of the rhythmic pattern of a musical composition into a cycle of a specified number of beats.

mediant - the tone between (the "medium" or halfway" tone) the tonic and its dominant (halfway between 1 and 5).

melody - the horizontal set of pitches organized in time that determines the shape of a musical line.

meter - the grouping of beats.

metered music - music that is grouped in a specific number of beats.

middle C - the ***C*** on the ledger line between the treble staff and the bass staff.

minor interval - interval of a 2nd, 3rd, 6th, or 7th that occurs naturally in the minor key of the root of the chord.

minor scale - a scale whose pattern of whole and half steps is: ***W***hole, ***H***alf, ***W***hole, ***W***hole, ***H***alf, ***W***hole, ***W***hole.

minor triad - a triad consisting of a minor 3rd, a major 3rd, and a perfect 5th.

monophony - music consisting of a single melodic line without additional parts or accompaniment.

Movable Do system - the solfege system used primarily in the United States, where ***Do*** moves to the tonic of each major key.

motive - the smallest distinctive melodic germ, made up of a few tones and rhythm.

music - sound and silence organized in time.

natural sign - a musical symbol that cancels a sharp or flat.

octave - the space (distance) between two notes of the same letter name; interval of an 8th.

Oktoechos - the "book of the eight tones", it is used in all musical traditions of the Orthodox Church.

passing tone - non-chord tone that moves by step between two different chord tones.

perfect interval - interval of a 1st, 4th, 5th, or 8th (octave) as it occurs naturally in the major key of the root of the chord.

phrase - the smallest complete melodic unit that can stand alone.

pick-up note - also called an ***anacrusis***, it is the beginning beat of a musical composition that does not begin on the first beat of the first full measure.

pitch - the highness or lowness of a sound resulting from vibrations per second.

plagal tones - tones (or modes) that correspond to another tone (or mode) whose number is referred to.

polyphony - music consisting of two or more independent melodies or lines.

preparation beat - a conducting signal to the singers which lets them when and how fast the music will begin, and that this is the moment to breathe.

Glossary of Terms 267

prokeimenon - meaning "introductory hymn", it serves to introduce the theme of the Epistle and Gospel lessons.

prokeimenon tones - tones set to the texts of the prokeimenon.

quarter note - a type of note composed of a blackened (filled-in) note head and a stem, and which, in common time, takes up one-fourth of a measure in $\frac{4}{4}$ time.

quarter rest - a rest shaped like a zig-zag, and which, in common time, takes up one-fourth of a measure in $\frac{4}{4}$ time.

recitative - reciting pitch; the pitch in the middle of a phrase on which are sung many words or syllables.

relative minor - the minor key that shares the same key signature as a corresponding major key.

rests - musical signs that denote silence.

root - the basic tone that serves as the generating force for other tones in the chord.

root position - a chord built with the root in the bass line.

rubrics - meaning "written in red", it refers to the descriptions and specifics of the structure of services; originally written in the service books in red ink.

SATB - designation for four-part singing, it refers to sopranos, altos, tenors, and basses.

scale - a series of ascending and descending tones, arranged in a pattern.

scale degrees - numerical names for the tones of a scale that classify their particular function within the scale.

second inversion - a chord with the 5th in the bass.

7th chord - a chord of four alternate pitches, consisting of a root, a 3rd, a 5th, and a 7th.

sharp - a musical symbol that raises the pitch of a note by one half step.

solfege syllables - the set of syllables for sight-singing: ***Do, Re, Mi, Fa, Sol, La, Ti, Do***.

solfege system - the system for using the solfege syllables for singing.

The Son - the eternal Son, Word, and Image of God, Who is the very Expression of the Being of the Father, and Who became incarnate as the man, Jesus Christ; the Second Person of the Holy Trinity.

staff - the set of lines and spaces on which music is written.

staves - the plural of "staff".

stikhera - verses.

stikhera style - a style of conducting stikhera that involves the use of the recitative and the cadence.

stikhera tones - tones used for the stikhera of such propers as "Lord, I Call" and the Apostikha at Vespers.

strict meter - meter having a strict number of beats for each measure.

sub-dominant - the tone a 4th above or a 5th below (the "under dominant") the tonic.

sub-mediant - the tone between (the "medium" or "halfway" tone) the sub-dominant and the tonic (halfway between 4 and 8).

subtonic - the 7th scale degree when it is a whole step below the tonic.

supertonic - the next tone above the tonic.

tenor - sustaining part.

theology - words adequate to God; the experience of our Faith, lived out in liturgy and in our daily lives.

third inversion - a 7th chord with the 7th in the bass.

3 pattern - a conducting pattern in which 3 beats are conducted in the following directional pattern: down, right, up.

time (meter) signature - the set of numbers at the beginning of a musical composition, showing how many beats there are per measure (the top number) and what type of note gets one beat (the bottom number).

tonic - tone of focus for the scale; the "home tone" of a key.

treble clef - also called the ***G-clef***, it is the symbol at the beginning of the treble staff.

treble staff - the upper staff of the grand staff, which covers the treble range of voices, those of sopranos and altos.

triad - a chord of three alternate pitches, consisting of a root, a 3rd, and a 5th.

troparion - a hymn whose theme is a specific saint or feast.

troparion tones - tones that are used to sing the troparion and kontakion, both resurrectional (for Sunday) and sanctoral (for the various saints and feasts).

2-pattern - a conducting pattern in which 2 beats are conducted in the following directional pattern: down, up.

upbeat - the second half of a beat.

whole note - a type of note composed of an open (not filled-in) note head without a stem, and which, in common time, takes up the whole measure in $\frac{4}{4}$ time.

whole rest - a rest which looks like an upside-down hat, and which, in common time, takes up the whole measure in $\frac{4}{4}$ time.

whole step - two half steps.

woodshedding - the gradual dissecting of the music down to its problem areas.

www.ingramcontent.com/pod-product-compliance
Lightning Source LLC
Chambersburg PA
CBHW050104170426
43198CB00014B/2452